CAPTURE *His* HEART

CAPTURE *His* HEART

Becoming the Godly Wife
Your Husband Desires

By Lysa TerKeurst

MOODY PRESS
CHICAGO

© 2002 by
LYSA TERKEURST

All Scripture quotations, unless otherwise indicated, are taken from the *Holy Bible New International Version®*, NIV®. Copyright © 1973, 1978, 1984 by International Bible Society. Used by permission of Zondervan Publishing House. All rights reserved.

Scripture quotations marked *The Message* are from *The Message*. Copyright © by Eugene H. Peterson 1993, 1994, 1995. Used by permission of NavPress Publishing Group.

Scripture quotations marked TLB are from *The Living Bible*, copyright © 1971. Used by permission of Tyndale House Publishers, Inc., Wheaton, IL 60189. All rights reserved.

Editorial services by: Julie-Allyson Ieron, Joy Media

Book design by: Julia Ryan [DesignByJulia]

ISBN: 0-8024-4040-1

3 5 7 9 10 8 6 4 2

Printed in the United States of America

ACKNOWLEDGMENTS: To Greg, Elsa, Bill, and the rest of the Moody Press staff: Thank you for catching the vision of the project. ■ *To Julie, Mark, and the rest of the Focus on the Family Publishing team: Thank you for helping carry the vision to many.* ■ To Julie-Allyson Ieron: Once again I thank you for lending your editorial expertise. ■ *To Marie Ogram: You are the world's greatest office manager and a wonderful friend. Thank you for all you did to make this project possible!* ■ To other staff members of Proverbs 31 Ministries–Sharon, Joel, Shelly, Sherry, Lisa, Glynnis, Carol, Linda, Miriam, Suzi, Falinda, Ann, and all the many volunteers: I couldn't do what I do without you. What a blessing to work with such first-class people. ■ *To Scott Gordon and team at Promise Keepers: Thank you for all your help surveying and compiling responses in preparation for this project.* ■ To the many couples who allowed me to peek inside your hearts and minds and benefit from the wonderful insights you provided, especially David and Becky, Steve and Sheila, Scott and Melanie, and Angee and Taz. ■ *To all the men and women who have their quotes published within these pages: Thank you and may God richly bless your marriage.*

To the man who has
captured my heart.
I love you, Art,
forever and ever.

*Also dedicated to the men and
women who want their marriages
to be pictures of Christ's grace,
mercy, and love. May these books
help you understand your mate
better and help you fall in love
all over again.*

THE GAME PLAN

Your husband needs you to enjoy him sexually.

Your husband needs you to appreciate him vocationally.

Your husband needs you to engage him intellectually.

Your husband needs you to connect with him relationally.

Your husband needs you to affirm him physically.

Your husband needs you to stand by him permanently.

WHAT THE HEART OF YOUR MAN WANTS YOU TO KNOW

T was weary from a long weekend of traveling and speaking. I was nearing the end of my trip and happy to reach my home airport. Only another hour and I'd be home, but first I had to go through the dreaded shuttle bus fiasco. I don't understand why I have such bad luck making it back to my car when I return home from trips. I am what you might call directionally challenged. Either I can't find the right bus or I can't find my car after the right bus drops me off. Anyhow, this shuttle bus dilemma was the last thing standing in my way to my journey home.

I exited the airport and to my surprise, the shuttle bus for my parking lot was waiting outside. Usually I have to wait an unreasonable amount of time for the shuttle, but not tonight. I was thrilled. I hauled my luggage up the bus stairs and greeted the driver with a big smile.

"You seem glad to see me," the driver said with a chuckle.

"I am," I happily replied.

"Yep, I sure do love my job," he said with a big grin and a southern twang. "Where else could a sixty-year-old man work where women are tripping over themselves to have me pick them up?"

I smiled politely and looked out the window.

He continued, "Yeah, everyone is excited to see me pull up to the curb. That's why I like my job so much. People get on the bus and smile so big. They've just been waiting for me, and when I finally arrive they are happy I'm here. I've often thought I wished I had a video camera to tape people as they get on my bus with their smiling faces and glad-to-see-ya' comments. I'd love for my wife to see a tape like that. That's the way I've always wanted her to look when I come home from work."

His story caught me by surprise. Something so simple would make such a huge impact on this man's marriage, and I bet his wife had no idea. I bet a lot of men have these simple desires, and I bet a lot of wives have no idea. I wondered what desires my husband had that I'd missed out on fulfilling. As I got off the bus I smiled and thanked the driver. My appreciation was for more than the ride to my car; he'd helped me find my way—my way on a journey to understanding the heart of my man.

After surveying hundreds of men, I found that there are eight basic concepts that the heart of your man wants you to know. They are:

1) Husbands need their wives to support them spiritually

2) Husbands need their wives to encourage them emotionally

3) Husbands need their wives to enjoy them sexually

4) Husbands need their wives to appreciate them vocationally

5) Husbands need their wives to engage them intellectually

6) Husbands need their wives to connect with them relationally

7) Husbands need their wives to affirm them physically

8) Husbands need their wives to stand by them permanently

I'm far from being the perfect wife, and I don't have a simple step-by-step method for a fail-proof marriage. What I do offer is a glimpse inside the hearts and minds of men. I have learned so much from the honest responses of guys who long to have their wives understand and appreciate them for the masculine beings they are.

Most of all, I've learned that a man desires his heart to be captured by his "Beauty," his lover, his friend, his partner through thick and thin. He wants to think about the times she told him he has what it takes. He takes great pride in knowing he makes her feel safe. He reflects on whether or not she thinks he's a good provider. And he dreams of the time when she initiated a passionate encounter and longs for another like it.

Men are fascinating. God made them that way. But many women find them frustrating and hard to figure out. I encourage you to put your frustrations and disappointments aside and set out on a journey of understanding, acceptance, and love for the heart of your beloved husband.

Proverbs 2:10–12 says, "For wisdom will enter your heart, and knowledge will be pleasant to your soul. Discretion will protect you, and understanding will guard you. Wisdom will save you from the ways of wicked men, from men whose words are perverse." That is my prayer for this book. I pray that wisdom will enter your heart and renew your commitment for your husband. I pray the knowledge will be pleasant to your soul and get your creativity flowing to make your marriage more special. I pray God will grant you discretion and understanding so you may be protected from the tragic statistics that plague the divine union of marriage.

Oh, and one more thing . . . I have to introduce you to Sabrina. She's a horrible woman who's been known to hold a grudge or two, accidentally on purpose oversalt her husband's eggs, and even to dump a glass of ice water on her husband in bed. She sometimes visits our home during "Princess Must Scream" (PMS) time. The bad thing is she looks just like me; in fact she is my alter ego—the Proverbs 31 woman in her not-so-finest hour. Throughout the book I'll share stories where I've succeeded in being a godly wife but I'll also share many of my failures. If my marriage could somehow make it through "Sabrina's" crazy antics, it gives hope that any marriage cannot only survive but truly thrive.

So won't you join me (and Sabrina) on this wild and wonderful adventure of better understanding our husbands as we seek to learn how to capture their hearts.

RELATIONSHIP BUILDER—*Find a unique way to tell your husband you love him today—make his coffee, warm his towel in the dryer, or as the quote below says: fluff his pillow.*

 THOUGHT FOR THE DAY—*It's the little things in life that make me happy—like when she fluffs my pillow before bed.—DON [WEST FRANKFORT]*

Your husband

needs you to

support him

spiritually.

CHAPTER 1

EVEN A GREAT HUSBAND
MAKES A POOR GOD

I got in my car and started down our winding driveway. Tears fell in a steady flow. My chest was tight, my eyes puffy, and every muscle tight with stress. *Why does it have to be so difficult? Why can't he just love me the way I am? Why does everything have to be such an issue? What am I doing wrong?*

Can you relate? If you've been married for any time at all, I'm sure you can. At times I've gotten so consumed trying to figure out how to make my husband love me and how to make everything all right between us that he in some strange way became my God. If we were doing well, I was doing well. If we weren't doing so well, I wasn't doing so well either.

Now, understandably, because my husband and I have come together as one, we are close enough that when he hurts, I hurt. But, my spirit should not vacillate between joy and sorrow based on how Art and I are getting along. Instead, my soul should always rest in the safety of Jesus' unconditional love and acceptance.

Jesus laid this principle out clearly in John 15:5–6, which says, "I am the vine; you are the branches. If a man remains in me and I in him, he will bear much fruit; apart from me you can do nothing. If anyone does not remain in me, he is like a branch that is thrown away and withers." Jesus is our life-giving vine; our husbands are not. If we remain in Christ and let Christ be the only one who holds our souls and determines our identity, then we can bear much fruit. We know from Galatians 5 that the fruit of God's Spirit in us is love, joy, peace, patience, kindness, goodness, faithfulness, gentleness, and self-control.

Can you see why it is so important to get your every deep, spiritual need met by God alone? My husband can't give me this type of consistent love, joy, peace, etc. And I can't give him love, joy, peace, patience, kindness, goodness, faithfulness, gentleness, and self-control apart from Christ. Apart from Christ I can do no good thing, because apart from Christ I wither as I try to make my husband fill me. When I do this I drain my husband and my marriage.

John 15:9 continues, "As the father has loved me, so have I loved you. Now remain in my love." Now, my sweet friend, I know what it is like to walk the rocky paths of a difficult marriage. I understand the loneliness, the desperation, the frustrations. But I also know what it's like to have a wonderful, fulfilling, romantic, awesome marriage.

My husband is basically the same man today as he was when things were not so good. God has worked on his heart and made some changes in him but nothing I've ever done had the power to change him. The main thing that has transformed my marriage is my letting God be my God. Instead of focusing on all the things my husband didn't do right or letting his approval and disapproval consume me, I learned to go to God and say, "Lord, I know You love me and You love my husband. So please either change him or change my heart toward this issue we are facing." Sometimes He'll soften my husband but more times than not God will change me.

 I often share at conferences and retreats that God has taught me what it means to live for an audience of one. Instead of trying to be a good wife to win my husband's approval, trying to be a good mom to win my kids' approval, and trying to be a good friend to win my friends' approval, I now simply try to please God. I seek only His favor and follow His precepts. In doing this I am a good wife, a good mom, and a good friend.

Faithfully spending time with God every day and asking Him to fill me and give me my identity and security has transformed my marriage. It has freed me to take the focus off of my needs, my wants, and my desires and turn more attention to giving of myself to my husband's needs, wants, and desires. It is only through God's strength working in me that I can give to my husband in this way and feel more fulfilled in giving than receiving.

Survey after survey that I received from men had a common thread: husbands said their wives were missing something in their life that the husbands had no idea how to fulfill. "I wish my wife knew that I love her," or "I want to give her what she needs but I'm not sure even she knows what that is," or "I wish so much my wife could see my inner feelings—how much I do love her—I just don't know how to make her see and believe that," and "I'm doing everything I know how to do to make her feel loved and it doesn't seem to be enough."

These husbands want their wives' hearts to be secure enough to freely receive the love they were already offering. The only way this can happen is when a wife's heart rests safely in the Lord's hands and she's at peace with who her God is. Then and only then can a woman of tender strength emerge with the capacity to be the wife she was created to be.

RELATIONSHIP BUILDER—*Spend time in prayer today asking God to change any wrong attitudes in your heart. Ask Him to make your marriage all He intends for it to be.*

 THOUGHT FOR THE DAY—*As the father has loved me, so have I loved you. Now remain in my love.*
—*[JOHN 15:9]*

CHAPTER 2

THE SUBMISSION MISSION

I know, I know, there's that word again: *submission*. Upon hearing it some women scowl, some smile, and others look puzzled. No matter what your initial reaction, I think you'll like the following article, condensed from one written by Curt Whalen, husband of a wife who learned a valuable lesson about submission. I think his words will touch your heart and possibly give you a new perspective on this subject.

Many women today desire a Christ-centered home. They keep their family involved in church, have regular family devotions, and spend time praying with their children. Yet while many women have hearts that long for the Lord, their husbands seem remote and distant. It was true for my wife, Marybeth. To an outsider looking into our lives, it would appear that I was as devoted to Christ as she was. Sadly, that wasn't true.

There was a time when God, the church, and my walk with Christ weren't important. I was a churchgoer (sometimes) and we had (she had) Christian friends, but I wasn't interested in getting closer to God than that. Daily prayer, Bible study, and intimate Christian fellowship were not part of my plan. My wife was the one trying to get our family to church. She scheduled our Christian activities. She reached out to others in need. But I was not her partner in these activities. In fact, I resented her love of God.

Looking back, I can see the pain I caused in her life. I remember looking into her eyes and seeing the hurt, sadness, and anger I caused. Now as I'm trying to grow closer to the Lord, I wonder how many other women have these same feelings. How many have husbands so devoted to their jobs that they check out of family life? How many wives have husbands who spend time absorbed in everything but their children? How many have husbands who have left home to pursue an adulterous relationship? How many women try to build a strong Christian family, yet feel defeated by the person who's supposed to be their spiritual partner?

I've got a long way to go in developing my relationship with Christ and with my wife, but slowly, with time, I've felt the hardness that surrounded my heart beginning to melt away. You might wonder how something like that could happen. The change in my life began simply. It began with a prayer.

In May 1996 my wife and I took our two kids to the beach for a week's vacation. She was pregnant, due in late July, and I was trying to give her that time to relax and enjoy herself before the baby came. While we were there, she was reading through a woman's devotional that led her to pray for three specific things. She prayed that my heart would turn towards the Lord, that our family would become

Christ-centered, and that God would break her heart with the things that break His.

Our family has experienced tremendous pain since that summer prayer. But through these times of hardship, I began to feel changes within myself. I felt a new desire to learn about the Lord. I began to reach out to God and wanted to learn everything I could about Him. I longed for Christ to not only fill my heart, but to change it. It seems so obvious now, but I began to understand that nothing is more important in this life than my personal relationship with the Lord, loving my wife, being a father to my children, and helping others in our church.

And it all started with the prayer of a woman whose heart longed for her family to follow Christ.

"Wives, in the same way be submissive to your husbands so that, if any of them do not believe the word, they may be won over without words by the behavior of their wives, when they see the purity and reverence of your lives" (1 Peter 3:1–2).

I can see how true this verse was in Marybeth's everyday living. She didn't try to talk me into following Christ. She lived it. And she prayed for me. She taught me of God's love and His grace during times when I'd terribly wounded her. She stood by me during times when people told her our marriage should end. Most importantly, she continued to pray for me during both the good and bad times.

To the wives who read this message and understand

the pain I discussed, please find words of encouragement. God loves you deeply and understands the pain in your heart. He loves your husband. He loves him for who he is, regardless of mistakes or sins. Our God is the loving father who every day scans the horizon searching for the prodigal son to appear so He can rush to him and embrace him and carry him home. God will hear your prayers. He longs to chip away at your husband's heart, just like He's been chipping away at mine.[1]

When I read his words my heart melted. When we follow God's pattern of submission, we draw our husbands' hearts to God. Let's reread that verse: "Wives, in the same way be submissive to your husbands so that, if any of them do not believe the word, they may be won over without words by the behavior of their wives, when they see the purity and reverence of your lives" (1 Peter 3:1–2). To be submissive does not mean to be a doormat and allow your husband to take advantage of you.

Cynthia Heald's definition is most vivid: "ducking low enough so God can touch your husband." When asked about submission, Cynthia said, "I went through a time when I was trying to get Jack to be more spiritual and do what I thought he should do as the leader in our home, and I was really frustrated because he wasn't doing those things. One day the Lord asked me if I was ready to give up with Jack and release him? And I said, 'No, I'm not. There are a couple more things I need to do yet.'" She went on to say, "It was a while before I was willing to say, 'Okay, God, he's yours.' Once I got out of the way God began to do incredible things in Jack's life—but not in my way or on my timetable."[2]

Marybeth learned that nagging Curt or rebelling against him would never help. So she, like Cynthia, turned her pleas over to the Lord. Slowly, the Lord changed Curt's heart and transformed a broken marriage. Though Marybeth would be quick to tell you her behavior was not always pure and reverent and her prayers were sometimes nothing more than heartbroken, tear-filled cries, she knew only God could change her husband. And eventually God did.

RELATIONSHIP BUILDER—*Submit to your husband today. Practice ducking low enough so God can touch your husband.*

 THOUGHT FOR THE DAY—*A woman will do whatever she can to control a man, but if she succeeds, she won't be happy.*—*[SUSAN YATES]*

CHAPTER 3

PRAYING FOR YOUR HUSBAND

In the last chapter we learned the mission of submission and how closely it ties into prayer. I know the power of prayer in a marriage. When my husband and I first married, we went through a terrible and hurtful adjustment period. We both brought lots of baggage from our pasts and expected the other to meet our needs and fix our hurts. Quickly, we both became overwhelmed and tired of not measuring up. We decided it was time to see a counselor. When that counselor couldn't help, we saw another and then another.

Finally, we wound up sitting across the desk from an older pastor who folded his hands, leaned back in his chair, and let out a deep sigh. He told us God was going to have to fix our individual hearts and then knit our hearts back together. I was stunned. I was looking for a quick and easy solution. I thought, *Come on, pastor, give us a three-step method to happiness.* He had no easy answers, and I left feeling hopeless.

That night I kept thinking about what he'd told us: "Let God fix your hearts individually and then God will knit your hearts back together." How could God do this? Our marriage was a mess. Love had been replaced with cold silence. Romance had been replaced with awkward coexistence. Bitterness and resentment had made both of us numb. Wouldn't it be better to call it quits? Surely another man out there would treat me better, understand my feelings, and meet my needs.

That's when God pierced my heart with a simple command, "Pray for Art." Pray? I had been praying. Hadn't God heard my cries of all that needed to be fixed with my husband? I had long lists that I presented to God and to Art on a regular basis. I kept waiting for a lightning bolt from heaven to hit him and show him the error of his ways. I'm sure he was waiting for the same for me. I thought God would "fix" him but instead God changed my heart. Now, when I'm praying for my marriage, more times than not I'm praying for God to give me the right heart attitude and the ability to respect my husband no matter what.

Stormie Omartian shares her experiences with how transforming prayer can be in a marriage in her best-selling book, *The Power of a Praying Wife*. She wrote:

> I began to pray every day for Michael (her husband), like I had never prayed before. Each time, though, I had to confess my own hardness of heart. I saw how deeply hurt and unforgiving of him I was. *I don't want to pray for him. I don't want to ask God to bless him. I only want God to strike him with lightning* (sound familiar?) *and convict him of how cruel he has been,* I thought. I had to say over and over, "God, I confess my unforgiveness toward my husband. Deliver me from all of it."
>
> Little by little, I began to see changes occur in both of us. When Michael became angry, instead of reacting

negatively, I prayed for him. I asked Him what I could do to make things better. He showed me. My husband's anger became less frequent and more quickly soothed. Every day, prayer built something positive. We're still not perfected, but we've come a long way. It hasn't been easy, yet I'm convinced that God's way is worth the effort it takes to walk in it.[1]

I believe in the power of praying scripturally for myself as a wife and for my husband. If you are not sure where to get started in praying for your marriage, let me encourage you to start with the prayers Stormie prayed.

Let me offer one last word of encouragement about the power of prayer in a marriage. I have never met a couple who prayed together on a regular basis who didn't have a healthy marriage. I'm not talking memorized ritual prayers. No, I'm talking about a couple who will kneel together before heaven's throne and pour out their hearts before the God of the universe. Praying together in this way will knit two hearts together like nothing else. If you've never prayed with your husband, start with short, simple prayers and ask God to show you both how to grow in this area of your oneness. If your husband does not feel comfortable praying out loud, then start by asking if the two of you could kneel together and pray silently. Then you pray fervently for God to give him the courage and you the wisdom to know how to encourage him in this area.

Everyone seems to be looking for a soulmate. I've heard

many couples splitting up because they've decided to go out and find their real soulmate. My friend, praying together as a couple will transform your relationship and make the two of you true "soulmates." I won't make many promises in this book, but this one I make without reservation: a couple that prays together, stays together!

RELATIONSHIP BUILDER—*Write personalized scriptural prayers for your husband today. Use the ones from this chapter to help get you started. Pray these for him often.*

 THOUGHT FOR THE DAY—*I have never met a couple who prayed together on a regular basis who didn't have a healthy marriage.*—*[LYSA TERKEURST]*

Your husband

needs you to

encourage him

emotionally.

CHAPTER 4

THE GREAT MASCULINE
ADVENTURE

D o you have a minute?" a woman asked as I left the podium and headed to the table in the back to sign books. She was quiet, yet I sensed her desperation.

"Of course," I replied.

"It's my husband; I can't respect him any longer, and I don't know what to do about it. I'm frustrated. Things have not been good between us for a long time. I want to give up but I know that's not the 'Christian' thing to do. I try. I do try but things never get better," she said with tears welling up in her eyes. I suspected not many of the other ladies attending the church retreat with her had any clue of her hurt by the way she kept her voice low and by her constant glances to make sure no one got close enough to hear our conversation.

My heart ached with this woman, for I knew her pain. The deep constant pain hidden behind the laughter and the perfect exterior. If ten women stood in a lineup and you were asked to pick out the one you thought might be on the brink of divorce, she'd be one of the last you'd pick. I was just like her once.

"You say you can't respect him?" I asked, hoping to get a glimpse of her pain's source.

"He's made so many mistakes and honestly I can't find a reason to respect him," she replied.

"While I don't know your circumstances, I do understand what it feels like to want to give up on your marriage. There was a time in my marriage when I wanted to give up too. But I didn't, because God gave me a verse that changed my perspective on marriage. Have you ever heard the verse where Jesus says, 'I tell you the truth, whatever you did for one of the least of these brothers of mine, you did for me' (Matthew 25:40)? That verse helped me understand that when I was so frustrated or angry at my husband that I couldn't respect him or show him kindness, he became a 'least of these brothers' in my eyes. Therefore this became an opportune time to do something precious for Jesus. When I love my husband when he's unlovable, I touch the heart of God."

Her eyes brightened. "Do you think you could take your husband out of the equation and look at respecting him as respecting Jesus or serving him as serving Jesus or even loving him as loving Jesus?" I asked.

"I think I can do that. Thank you," she said as she wiped her tears, lifted her head, and walked away.

We may never know how personally Jesus takes our actions toward our husbands but I do know this: When I look at serving, loving, or respecting my husband as doing it for Jesus, my attitude changes. It's as if God spoke to my heart with this verse and forever changed my perspective.

Listen to how God changed the heart of Sister Mary Rose McGready, president of Covenant House—America's largest shelter for homeless children. She wrote in her book, *Please Help Me God,* "On the street I saw a small girl shivering in a thin dress, with little hope of a decent meal. I became angry and said to God: 'Why do you permit this? Why don't you do something about it?' And God replied, 'I certainly did do something about it. I made you.'"[1]

We say our husbands aren't understanding. We say they aren't sensitive. We have long lists of how our husbands fall short. God certainly did do something about this: He created us! Remember the Garden of Eden? The only time God said something was not good while creating the heavens and earth was in Genesis 2:18, which says, "The LORD God said, 'It is not good for the man to be alone. I will make a helper suitable for him.'" So the Lord created the woman to be man's suitable helper—to help him become all God intended him to be.

Joel, one of the men I interviewed in preparation for this book, gave me great insight on this. He said, "Ask wives what they wish their husbands would be: a better spiritual leader? more compassionate? a better father? a better provider? Start building upon what's already there by showing respect and giving encouragement. Maybe he prays once over a family meal; build on that. From there he could become a great spiritual leader."

Proverbs 31:10–12 says, "A wife of noble character who can find? She is worth far more than rubies. Her husband has full confidence in her and lacks nothing of value. She brings him good, not harm, all the days of her life." Verse 23 continues,

"Her husband is respected at the city gate, where he takes his seat among the elders of the land." What might your husband become with your respect, support, and encouragement? Giving your husband respect whether he deserves it or not pleases God and transforms husbands. It has worked wonders in my marriage.

RELATIONSHIP BUILDER—*Have a servant's heart and attitude today. Look for ways to serve your husband as you would Jesus.*

 THOUGHT FOR THE DAY—*A wife of noble character who can find? She is worth far more than rubies. Her husband has full confidence in her and lacks nothing of value. She brings him good, not harm, all the days of her life.*
—*[PROVERBS 31:10–12]*

CHAPTER 5

TOUCHING THE HEART
OF YOUR TENDER WARRIOR

I 'll never forget the day I realized my husband had tender places inside. His exterior seemed so tough and self-assured, that I forgot he had feelings. I thought I was the only one with emotions in our relationship. I was wrong. My husband is a tender warrior, fully masculine yet with feelings that can and do get hurt, even crushed.

Think of David from the Bible. This brave young man stepped up to fight Goliath when none of the other warriors would. He had nothing but a slingshot, five smooth stones, and a heart for God. As the giant mocked and threatened, David replied to the Philistine:

> You come against me with sword and spear and javelin, but I come against you in the name of the LORD Almighty, the God of the armies of Israel, whom you have defied. This day the LORD will hand you over to me, and I'll strike you down and cut off your head. Today I will give the carcasses of the Philistine army to the birds of the air and the beasts of the earth, and the whole world will know that there is a God in Israel. All those gathered here will know that it is not by sword or spear that the LORD saves; for the battle is the LORD's, and he will give all of you into our hands (1 Samuel 17:45–47).

We know from Sunday school that David slung one of his rocks knocking Goliath in his forehead killing him instantly. This story makes me want to stand up and cheer: "Go, David, go!" He's so brave and sure of God's presence and faithfulness.

Then my thoughts turn to another side of David. The side where his tender feelings were revealed. Where his tough, assured exterior melted away and his vulnerability surfaced. In Psalm 31 David cried out to God:

> In you, O LORD, I have taken refuge; let me never be put to shame; deliver me in your righteousness. Turn your ear to me, come quickly to my rescue; be my rock of refuge, a strong fortress, to save me. Since you are my rock and my fortress for the sake of your name lead and guide me. Free me from the trap that is set for me, for you are my refuge. Into your hands I commit my spirit; redeem me, O LORD, the God of truth . . .
>
> Be merciful to me, O LORD, for I am in distress; my eyes grow weak with sorrow, my soul and my body with grief. My life is consumed by anguish and my years by groaning; my strength fails because of my affliction, and my bones grow weak (1–5, 9–10).

I am convinced after reading through all the surveys I collected that the place from where David pours out these vulnerable feelings exists in every man. Here are a few of those comments:

"I am afraid of my weaknesses and am unable to communicate

these fears adequately."—ANONYMOUS [CHARLOTTE, NC]

"I have tender feelings that are sometimes crushed by joking words or times of no attention."—PHILLIP [SUMMERFIELD]

"Even though I put on a tough armor daily, I feel it is to protect my soft heart."—ANONYMOUS

"As much as women want their emotional needs to be met, so do I. I love to be held, loved, adored, and desired emotionally. I am not just a coworker in the house."—ANONYMOUS

In *Four Pillars of a Man's Heart* Stu Weber writes,

> The influence of applied femininity is, by any measure, incredibly determinative. In every culture, in every age, the power is awesome. And dangerous. As with any significant reservoir of power it may be used for good or ill. Its impact may be constructive or destructive. Like a mighty river, it is a force that may turn the turbines and generate power that will light up a community, a home, and a man's whole life. But undisciplined and unchecked, it may devastate, demoralize, and utterly destroy.
>
> Some women have no clue how much actual power they hold, and those are the women who destroy their husbands by default. Other women are acutely aware of their power and make a conscious decision to become high controllers. But still other women, keenly aware of

the power God has vested in their femininity, make a deliberate choice to use that power only for good.[1]

I'll never forget the day I saw my husband's feelings crushed by the weight of my careless words. I saw the "power" Stu Weber described being used for harm and it shocked me. I never knew I could have such an impact on my husband. I now know if I really want to capture the heart of my man, I've got to make understanding his tender spots a priority. And more than just understanding, I need to give him the support that says, "I believe in you." That's what I now know is key to touching the heart of my tender warrior.

RELATIONSHIP BUILDER—*Use your words to build up your husband today. Tell him something you know his heart longs to hear from you. You may even want to ask for his forgiveness for using your words carelessly in the past.*

 THOUGHT FOR THE DAY—*Even though I put on a tough armor daily, I feel it is to protect my soft heart.*
—*ANONYMOUS*

CHAPTER 6

BOYS WILL BE BOYS

I get scared every time I walk into our toolshed. There are creatures big and small that have taken up residence in this dark and musky place. *I wonder if we might paint the walls and accessorize the rugged decor. Maybe a potted plant growing out of a boot and a wreath with a little greenery?* It is power tool and gadget Grand Central Station. There's a tractor, a lawn mower, attachments for the tractor, attachments for the lawn mower, a weed whacker, a trimmer thingie, and other sharp and dangerous gadgets. *Can we put some kind of protective coverings over all these blades? I even put a plastic sheath over my pizza cutter for fear of reaching into the utensil drawer and cutting my finger. One little fall in this place, and you could lose an entire limb.* And the smell . . . a pungent mixture of gasoline and sweat. *Potpourri anyone?*

When my husband walks into "his place," he smiles. Picture Tim the Tool-Man Taylor letting out one of his "Aarrrgh, Aarrgh, Aarrgh" laughs when he flexes his muscles and cranks up his power tools. He loves the smell, doesn't notice the creatures, and the sharp edges invite the right element of danger and adventure to make the setting perfectly suited for him. This is his place to fully express his masculinity and be the man. That's what most men really want to be: the man.

John Eldridge in his book, *Wild at Heart*, revealed something amazing to me about my husband's desire to be the man. Eldridge writes,

> There are three desires I find written so deeply into my heart I know now I can no longer disregard them without losing my soul. They are core to who and what I am and yearn to be. I gaze into boyhood, I search the pages of literature, I listen carefully to many, many men, and I am convinced these desires are universal, a clue into masculinity itself. They may be misplaced, forgotten, or misdirected, but in the heart of every man is a desperate desire for a battle to fight, an adventure to live, and a beauty to rescue.[1]

I grew up in a household of women. My poor dad had five girls, a southern belle wife, and a female toy poodle named "Biscuit." Dad spent a lot of time hunting and fishing during certain times each month. When I had babies it was no shock to have three girls. Then my sister Angee kept the trend going with her first child: a girl. Fifteen months later our family's world changed when she welcomed her second child: a boy. Complete with karate chops, sword fights, and a wrestle-mania attitude, this little creature educated us all that boys will be boys. He wanted to be the warrior and the hero.

These desires are deeply embedded in my husband and yours as well. And it's not enough to just want to be the man of adventure and heroics; he wants someone to do it all for. He wants a beauty who thinks he's the hero and is woman enough to tell him. My husband lights up when I build him up by telling him he's strong and he makes me feel safe at night. Or when he goes off fishing with the boys and is welcomed home with words like, "How are you so smart when it comes to all this fishing stuff?" and, "I love it when you look so rugged."

 Stepping out on the edge of masculinity where danger and adventure lie is what men are longing for today, and yet too many of us wives are holding them back in the name of responsibility and maturity.

Interestingly enough, Eldridge points out that the result of holding a man back from being the man is: "Women are often attracted to the wilder side of a man, but once having caught him they settle down to the task of domesticating him. Ironically, if he gives in he'll resent her for it, and she in turn will wonder where the passion has gone. Most marriages wind up there. A weary and lonely woman asked me the other day, 'How do I get my husband to come alive?' 'Invite him to be dangerous,' I said."[2]

Understand that it is important for a man to help around

41

the house and with the kids. In fact in the husband's companion to this book, I told him that one of the best ways to romance his wife is by helping her. But, there's got to be a balance. A man has to have time to go off to a masculine adventure where his testosterone can kick into high gear and his adrenaline surge. For some men it will be the great outdoors where he can fish, hunt, rock climb, or explore. For others it will be in the world of sports or farming or woodworking. Whatever his chosen adventure may be, encourage his participation and let him know you support him and are even attracted to his wild side.

Back to that toolshed. I've stopped thinking of ways to bring feminine touches to this place. I've stopped telling him he shouldn't ride such dangerous equipment. Some kings mount great stallions to ride into battle, others their Harley Davidson motorcycles. Mine rides into the sunset on a Massey Furgeson Tractor.

RELATIONSHIP BUILDER—*Catch your husband doing something masculine today and tell him how attracted you are to his wild side.*

 THOUGHT FOR THE DAY—*Several years ago* Time *magazine featured an article titled, "Men: Are They Really That Bad?" where author Lance Morrow concluded that "the overt man bashing of recent years has now . . .*

settled down to a vague male aversion, as if masculinity were a bad smell in the room."[3] *How sad. I say, real women love real men—masculinity and all.*

Your husband needs you to enjoy him sexually.

CHAPTER 7

THE MAKINGS OF A
BETTER LOVER

Sex. Just mention the word in a crowd of women and in and among the snickers and giggles, you'll get a wide range of reactions. Some will roll their eyes. Some will smile. Some will frown. Some are willing to jump right into conversation. Some will have no comments at all.

When I surveyed women across the country for *Capture Her Heart: Becoming the Godly Husband Your Wife Desires,* I got a huge response concerning sex. Most comments centered around how to romance a woman. Typical comments were "helping me around the house is foreplay," "realize I can't go from cleaning toilets and wiping noses to sex goddess in 30 seconds or less," and "women need to feel emotionally attached before being physically connected."

It will come as no surprise that sex was on the minds of the men surveyed as well. Listen to some of the comments given:

"I need to feel the reinforcement of her touch. When she touches me out of her own effort, my world comes alive! When she touches me I can understand how Christ felt about the church . . . how He could die for her."—MATT [HOPKINSVILLE]

"I need romantic and enthusiastic sex."—Anonymous

"I wish my wife could understand how important it is for me to have her desire marital intimacy with me. I'm not talking about just the physical act but the need to know that she desires to be intimate with me."—Jimmy [Indian Trail]

Do you see a common thread? Words like *effort, enthusiastic,* and *desire* were common. Our husbands want us to want them sexually.

Too many times in the past when my husband approached me with that look . . . you know the one I'm talking about . . . I would think, *Not tonight.* I would count the days since we were last together and try to make the call as to whether or not his need was justifiable. I realize in some marriages the roles are reversed where the woman desires intimacy more than her husband but bear with me here, there's good information for you too.

Sexual intimacy is more than meeting a physical need. It is the most vulnerable way to let your spouse know he is wholly desirable and accepted. Think back to the Garden of Eden. In Genesis 2:25 it states, "The man and his wife were both naked, and they felt no shame." They had absolute confidence in their commitment to one another. They totally accepted and trusted each other.

Your husband longs for this. When he makes himself vulnerable, he longs to know you will find him desirable and acceptable. When a man makes a sexual advance toward his wife, it is more than just a desire to be physically involved. He's offering a question that his heart wants answered: "Do I have what it takes to be a real man and satisfy you in a deep and intimate way?"

If the wife says yes and reciprocates his touch with as much excitement as he offers it, his masculinity comes alive and is affirmed deeply. If she says no, it hurts physically and emotionally. Physically, it opens him to a world of temptation when his sexual needs are not met regularly. Emotionally, he seeks to aggressively prove he has what it takes in other areas of life to make up for the lack of intimate approval.

To take this a step further, if a wife initiates a sexual experience, it sets his heart on fire. Think about when your husband takes the initiative to plan a special date night for the two of you. Doesn't it mean more than if you have to ask him to take you on a date? Dane from Charlotte said, "Though agreeing to a 'quickie' because she looked at the calendar and realized it's been a while since we fluffed the feather bed is fine sometimes, it does a man's ego a lot of good for his wife to be the initiator of a nontimed event." He is not alone in his desire.

 Let me encourage you to seek to find out what is holding you back from being the sexual partner your husband longs for. Pray and ask God to reveal any wrong attitude or misconception about His beautiful gift of intimacy. Ask God for a renewed desire for your husband. Fill your mind with beautiful Scriptures from the Song of Solomon. Read helpful Christian books on this subject. One written by women for women that I would recommend is *Intimate Issues* by Linda Dillow and Lorraine Pintus (WaterBrook Press).

Think back to your dating days when you found your husband irresistible and resurrect those thoughts. Make a list of all the qualities that attract you to your husband and think about those things often. Determine to not base your desire for intimacy on your husband's efforts or lack of effort to romance you. Remember, we can't control our husband or make him do what we want; we can, however, make good choices ourselves.

Do whatever it takes to put yourself in a romantic frame of mind. Take a bubble bath. Put on your favorite perfume. Treat yourself to a manicure. Play romantic music. Light some candles. If you are tired, find time to take a nap. If you lack energy, eat better and exercise more. If the kids are little and time-consuming, get a sitter or trade out with a friend. Remember whatever you put into your marriage is what you'll get out of it. These little things are wise investments for your relationship.

Before you start rolling your eyes and saying I don't understand, trust me, I do. I've had to make a mind-shift in the way I approach my marriage bed. But my marriage is better than it has ever been. I now love being intimate with my husband. And the more fulfilled he is in his needs, the more fulfilled I am in mine.

RELATIONSHIP BUILDER—*Make a list of the qualities that attract you to your husband. Pray that God would give you a desire to initiate an intimate experience with your husband.*

 THOUGHT FOR THE DAY—*Like an apple tree among the trees of the forest is my lover among the young men. I delight to sit in his shade, and his fruit is sweet to my taste.*—[SONG OF SOLOMON 2:3]

CHAPTER 8

AN AMAZING BANQUET

In a scene from a movie, a husband and wife are shown each talking with a therapist. On the left half of a split screen, the man complains, "We hardly ever have sex. Maybe three times a week, tops." On the right half of the screen the woman laments, "We are constantly having sex. We must have it three times a week!"

This dialogue is consistent with the age-old tension that exists between many husbands and wives. What is it that drives most men to desire a sexual encounter every couple of days, and why is it that most women need the romantic experience of emotional connection more than the physical connection?

Simply stated, why is it that most women want physical intimacy less often and men more often? I realize this is not true for some couples. However, for those that it is true this issue causes real problems that need to be addressed. Bob and Rosemary Barnes in their book, *Rock Solid Marriage,* give helpful insights, "Biology is only one part of the formula for the male sex drive. . . . But there's more than the biology. Men are stimulated or triggered by sight. They respond to visual stimuli."[1]

We live in a sexual image-saturated society. You can't drive down the road and not see a billboard with some type of sexual innuendo. You can't go to the gas station or the neighborhood grocery store without seeing scantily clad women staring back at you from the covers of magazines. *Sports Illustrated* dedicates one whole issue a year to women in swimsuits . . . and trust me it's not so women can see what the latest fashion will be for swimwear. Men respond to visual stimuli and the world we live in bombards our husbands daily. "The fact that a man is visually stimulated cannot be overlooked by a wife. She needs to understand her husband and do what she can to help him 'rejoice in the wife of [his] youth' (Proverbs 5:18)."[2]

One night my husband and I were having this "frequency" discussion. I was trying to paint a word picture to help him understand that just because I didn't want to make love at times didn't mean I didn't love him. I explained that as a mother of young children I'm on touch overload by the time I go to bed. It's as if I were full and someone placed my favorite dish in front of me and told me to eat up and enjoy. While I might love this meal, I'm too full to partake.

Art listened intently. Then he painted his own version of this word picture. In his version, he hadn't had anything to eat in several days and was famished. Then someone placed his favorite meal in front of him but instructed him he must only look, not partake.

How can we resolve this and enjoy God's gift of sexual intimacy? Romance has a lot to do with it. To continue my word picture, a wife needs to be made hungry again. Most women will only long to be touched sexually if they feel filled emotionally.

But not all husbands are naturally romantic. Since we can't

change our husbands or control what they may or may not be willing to do, let's talk about something we can do to get filled up emotionally and help our sexual appetite: rekindle our first love.

 I wish I could say I was a virgin when I got married, but I wasn't. I experienced sexual abuse from a grandfather figure and rejection from my biological father before most kids even know those words exist. All of these negative experiences had a negative effect on the way I approached my marriage bed. Old tapes of bad experiences would play in my head and interrupt the tenderness between Art and me.

Maybe you, too, faced situations similar to mine, and sex has become a dirty word. Let me encourage you to take these feelings to God. Let Him heal you and give you a new view of sexual intimacy. I love the Scripture that says, "Therefore, if anyone is in Christ, he is a new creation; the old has gone, the new has come!" (2 Corinthians 5:17).

God can make a way for us, too, to forget the things of the past and experience the new and sweet intimacy He intends for sexual relations with our husbands. For me, when I rekindled my love with God and sought to understand what the Scriptures tell us about sex, my desire to be sexually intimate with my husband was rekindled.

God's Word tells us sex is incredible. Genesis 4:1 in the King James Version tells us that it allows a husband and wife to "know" each other sexually. This kind of intimate knowledge between a husband and a wife connects two people physically, emotionally, and spiritually. Genesis 2:24 says, "A man will leave his father and mother and be united to his wife, and they will become one flesh." This is a beautiful picture of two becoming one in the most intimate of ways in God's eyes. God doesn't refer to sex as bringing a couple close or even connected. He refers to it as becoming one. Beautiful benefits come from this oneness. It creates life and amazing pleasure.

I remember being awed when each of our children was born. Our love created three of the most beautiful blessings I've ever seen. Out of our love, God allowed a part of Art and a part of me to join Him in creating life. What an amazing thing! God made our bodies to fit together just right and for each to contain half of what is needed for life to be created.

Making love can also provide intense and wonderful pleasure. Let your desire be only for the amazing man God has given you as your husband. Song of Solomon 4:9–10 says, "You have stolen my heart, my sister, my bride; you have stolen my heart with one glance of your eyes, with one jewel of your necklace. How delightful is your love, my sister, my bride! How much more pleasing is your love than wine, and the fragrance of your perfume than any spice!" Intoxicate your husband with the sweet pleasure only you can provide him and at the same time allow yourself the wonderful experiences of sexual arousal and pleasure.

By rekindling your love for God and His Word and seeking His perfect design for sexual intimacy, your marriage bed can become more fulfilling than ever.[3]

RELATIONSHIP BUILDER—*Write 2 Corinthians 5:17 on a note card and put it in your purse. For the next week every time you find yourself waiting in traffic, at a store, at the doctor's office, pull that card out and pray that God would give you a renewed desire for being physically intimate with your husband.*

THOUGHT FOR THE DAY—*Most women want to know if their sex life is normal. So, they pick up* Reader's Digest *and read an insightful article about sexual frequency in marriage. . . . Not most men! We're not interested in* Reader's Digest *or in averages. If sexual frequency is the issue, we want the* Guinness Book of World Records! *. . . Who wants to be average? Let's go for the gold!*—[ROBERT LEWIS AND WILLIAM HENDRICKS][4]

CHAPTER 9

ENCOUNTER OR EXPERIENCE?

A third major concern that kept coming up in the surveys was that husbands wished their wives would enjoy their sex life more. Jay from Charlotte says, "It would be helpful for a wife to understand the benefits to her in seeking to meet her husband's sexual needs. My wife and I have friends that really seem to get this. Every day she asks her husband if she 'can help.' They are in their late forties. Interestingly enough, he gladly looks for ways to meet her needs like no other husband I know."

A man needs to know that sex is on the mind of his wife. And what ultimately fulfills a man once in bed even more than his own sexual release is knowing he has provided his wife the same pleasure. Yet many women struggle with fully enjoying intimate connections with their husbands.

God intended both men and women to become aroused and experience the full richness of climaxing within the bond of marriage. For most men the full cycle of arousal, erection, encounter, and release is done almost without thought. It is a physical drive. For most women the process is more complicated. A woman usually wants an experience, not just a sexual encounter with her husband. She needs and wants to be emotionally, mentally, and physically stimulated culminating in a lovemaking experience.

EMOTIONALLY FILLING

When a man is emotionally drained, a sexual encounter with his wife can do more to lift his spirits than almost anything else. His emotions are driven by feeling like the man and feeling like he has what it takes to be the man. A woman is different. If a woman is down emotionally, the last thing she wants is to be physically connected. She needs to be emotionally filled. So what do you do if your husband is not doing a good job of filling your emotional tank? Let God fill it. I don't want to sound trite, but ultimately only God can fill your emotional need.

 At the core of a woman's emotions she wants to know, "Am I lovely?" and "Am I loved?" The unconditional love our hearts long for can only be found in a personal relationship with the great lover of our souls, Jesus Christ. Even the best husband can't give a woman everything she needs to be satisfied emotionally. In letting Jesus fill our empty emotional places, we then have love to give. The miracle of it all is that in getting on our knees and asking God to fill us, reassure us, and lavish His love on us, not only do we have love to give but we can more confidently receive whatever love our husbands give us.

An emotionally confident and secure woman can look at sex in a whole new light. It is a delight to be physically connected to her husband. She is able to let herself be vulnerable and naked without emotional reservation.

ENJOYING SEX MENTALLY

A woman's largest sexual organ is found in her mind. If making love is viewed as a dreaded chore, it will be difficult for it to be pleasurable. If a woman has a million things running through her mind and a zillion more on her to-do list, it's difficult to shift into a romantic frame of mind. More so if a woman focuses only on the negative aspects of her husband, it will be difficult to want a close physical relationship with him.

Dr. Douglas Rosenau in his book *A Celebration of Sex* says that making love is 80 percent fantasy (imagination and mind) and about 20 percent friction (physical touch and connection). As women, the power of our state of mind towards love-making is crucial and developing a healthy fantasy life is essential. By healthy I mean fantasies that focus your attention only on your husband and that which enhances your sex life within your marriage. Dr. Rosenau says, "You can rid yourself of old messages that you must maintain control and never be passionate. You can unleash the playful and sexy parts of yourself as you romp with your mate with a renewed attitude. You can also purge your mind of any thoughts that might get in the way of uninhibited lovemaking with your mate—lustful thoughts of another person, a preoccupation with job or children, the idea that sex is dirty. . . . You can prepare for action and have a creative sexual mind-set that will result in enticing, dynamic lovemaking."[1]

This is possible when we seek to fill our minds with loving thoughts and satisfying mental pictures of our husband. Always thinking there is someone else out there who might better meet your needs is dangerous. I've spoken to women who struggle with being attracted to a friend's husband or another man with whom they come in contact. Maybe this man compliments her often and says things she wishes her husband would say.

That other man has his many flaws and shortcomings. Chances are you are not really attracted to this other person but rather to the excitement that comes with something new and different. God has given you the gift of your husband because he is right for you and you for him.

You can discover a renewed excitement in your relationship. Dr. Rosenau says that within your marriage it is possible to find newness and adventure that will greatly enhance your relationship. "The human mind is curious and loves mystery or new experiences. Your imaginative capacity and fantasy can help fulfill this in many ways. Keep an adventurous component in your personality. Fantasy with mystery and novelty can give your love life wings."[2]

ENJOYING SEX PHYSICALLY

"It is obvious that God intended for a woman to experience tremendous physical pleasure in marital lovemaking. He provided a specific point of pleasure at creation. We know of no other reason for that little organ, about a centimeter in size, above the opening to a woman's vagina. It is called the clitoris, and it's there for sexual arousal."[3] While a man's sexual organs are obvious, a woman's are not so obvious. Have you and your husband ever spent time talking about what does and does not make you feel comfortable, aroused, and sensually stimulated? Let me encourage you to pray for the courage to do so.

To truly get to know your husband and for him to truly know you, you will have to spend time communicating and exploring this awesome gift from God together. Guide your husband's hands to touch you where it brings you pleasure. Show him how to be tender in some places and aggressive in others as he caresses you and holds you. Tell him where you enjoy his kisses. The more you communicate and open yourself up to your husband, the more he can understand how to truly satisfy you and the more satisfied he will be as well.

Making love with your husband can and should be wonderfully exciting and amazingly pleasurable. Ask God today to help you enjoy His amazing gift with your husband emotionally, mentally, and physically. Take time to discover a renewed passion and desire for making your marriage bed all that it should be.

RELATIONSHIP BUILDER—*Schedule a night this week when you and your husband can spend some quiet intimate time together talking about what is pleasurable to you both and explore this awesome gift of making love to its fullest satisfaction.*

 THOUGHT FOR THE DAY—*The wife's body does not belong to her alone but also to her husband. In the same way, the husband's body does not belong to him alone but also to his wife.—[1 CORINTHIANS 7:4]*

Your husband

needs you to

appreciate him

vocationally.

CHAPTER 10

YOUR PROVIDER: PUFFED UP
OR POOPED OUT

I 've met millionaires whose wives are dissatisfied with the way their husbands provide. I've also met people who live below poverty level and yet their spouses seem content. What makes the difference, and how can a marriage escape the money problems that plague so many relationships? The secret again lies in perspective.

In Philippians 4:12 Paul says, "I know what it is to be in need, and I know what it is to have plenty. I have learned the secret of being content in any and every situation, whether well fed or hungry, whether living in plenty or in want." Then in verse 13 he gives us the secret: "I can do everything through him who gives me strength."

The *NIV Life Application Study Bible* commentary says:

> Are you content in any circumstances you face? Paul knew how to be content whether he had plenty or whether he was in need. The secret was drawing on Christ's power or strength. Do you have great needs, or are you discontented because you don't have what you want? Learn to rely on God's promises and Christ's power to help you be content. If you always want more ask God to remove that

desire and teach you contentment in every circumstance. He will supply all your needs, but in a way that he knows is best for you. . . . Paul was content because he could see life from God's point of view. He focused on what he should do, not what he felt he should have.[1]

Keeping our perspective like Paul's will help us not to pressure our husbands or question their provision. Now that we know how not to "poop out" our provider, how do we help puff him up and encourage him in this role?

 I was interviewing a couple of men on Wednesday night before our church service began and asked what encourages them in their role as provider. One was quick to respond, "When my wife greets me at the door after a long day at the office dressed in a way that lets me know she's thinking about the same thing I am." The other man said, "What encourages me in my role as provider is when she tells me that she thinks I'm smart. In times past she's said she loves the way I handle things and that she thinks I have a good business sense. I don't feel very smart, but knowing that she thinks I am lifts my spirits."

His words challenged me. When was the last time I told my provider I think he's smart? Or that he's a great provider? I think most husbands would benefit from hearing these words. Maybe too many husbands instead have heard words that deflated and discouraged them: "Why don't we ever have enough money?" or "If only you were a better money manager," or "It sure would be nice to live like the Johnsons; they never have to worry about money," or "If only you'd finished your degree, then we'd have more money and we wouldn't be in this mess."

Every weekday my provider heads off to a world full of people waiting to beat him up. Customers aren't satisfied. Managers question performance. Bosses beat on the door wanting to know why the bottom line isn't improving. Computers crash. Workers quit. Some of you ladies may say, "I work in an office with the same kinds of stresses you just described. What about me?" Or others of you may say, "I'd trade places with him any day of the week. I face screaming toddlers, dirty diapers, piles of laundry, and soap scum." I know you might feel this way because I've had those same feelings. But we'll never get anywhere having our pity parties. Our marriage will never improve if we think only of ourselves. We will, however, make great strides if we seek to lovingly give to our mate.

SO HERE IS MY PUFF UP YOUR PROVIDER LIST

■ Send a thank you card to your husband's work address telling him how much you appreciate all he does.

■ Ask him if there is anything you could do for him today that would take a little stress off of him.

■ Tell him he's smart.

■ Call him in the middle of the day and tell him that you are thinking of him and can't wait until he gets home.

■ See how much money you can save this month by cutting back on groceries, clipping coupons, making fewer trips to places where you find you spend too much money, and eating out less.

■ Make it a point this month to determine not to complain about money or the lack thereof not even once.

■ Try greeting him at the door dressed in a way that tells him you've been thinking the same thing he has all day.

■ What are some other practical ways to puff up your provider?

RELATIONSHIP BUILDER—*Take your calendar out and write across the top of it, "No $ Complaints," to help you remember your no-complaining commitment this month. Then schedule a couple of the other ideas from the list to implement throughout the next couple of weeks. Maybe you even want to go through the rest of this year's calendar and make some of these ideas and others you think of a part of your regular routine.*

 THOUGHT FOR THE DAY—*Send the kids to stay overnight with their grandparents, cook your husband's favorite meal, light some candles, wear something that doesn't completely hide everything, and then let nature take its course and delight in each other. . . . Meet him at the door with nothing on some time. (Just make sure it's not the UPS man.) I can't describe what a thrill it would be for him to know you can have some fun, too.*—*[CHUCK SNYDER]*[2]

CHAPTER 11

DON'T CLIP HIS WINGS

I 've heard different versions of this story passed around through the years. City councilman Pete and his wife, Nancy, were taking a walk through a construction site of a new city building. They were admiring the fine architecture when one of the construction workers cried out, "Hey, Nancy, remember me—we used to date in high school." Nancy instantly recognized her old friend and went over to say hello. After they walked away, Pete said, "Nancy, aren't you glad you married me? If you would have married that guy, you would have been the wife of a construction worker." Nancy smiled back and replied, "If I would have married him, he would have been a city councilman."

The influence a wife has on her husband is great. You've heard the expression before, "Behind every great man is a great woman." Most every man wishes he had a great woman behind him. One who believes in him, builds him up, supports him and encourages him no matter if his lifelong dream is to be a construction worker or a city councilman.

One man on his survey responded, "I wish my wife could understand that I am a work in progress: God is not through with me so keep praying." Another said, "Please be easy with advice." To appreciate our husbands vocationally, we would all do well to keep those comments in mind. I titled this chapter,

"Don't Clip His Wings," because I'm convinced wives have no idea the influence they have on their husbands. We can either help our husbands rise to what God has purposed for them or we can clip their wings so they never even get off the ground. It is a great honor and privilege to be a husband's helpmate.

To understand how to help and not hinder our husbands, there are four important steps we can take.

 FIRST we must take into consideration how we offer our help. Too many times I've blasted my husband with a "my way or the highway" advice session. Once he looked at me hurt and overwhelmed by my attempts to "help" and said, "Since you are obviously wearing the pants, do you want the belt too?" I realized there is a right way and wrong way to help, and I was not choosing wisely. Now, before I offer any advice I let him finish what he is saying. Sometimes, he's looking to share something to get it off his chest, and he's not looking for anything more than a listening ear. If I think advice is called for, I try to offer it in a gentle spirit of love and phrase it in non-finger-pointing ways.

THE SECOND STEP toward being your husband's wise helper is to understand his greatest fear. "On a number of occasions I have heard that a woman's greatest fear is that something will happen to one of her children. Men, of course, fear this too. A man's most conscious fear, however, is that he will not be able to provide for his family."[1] In an effort to conquer this fear, a man heads off to the rat race and then comes face-to-face with one of the most pivotally defining moments of his life: will work consume me or will I keep my priorities in balance? We must make sure we're not putting added pressure on him to provide more and bigger and better. We must also make sure that home is a place he wants to come to, a place where he feels needed, wanted, respected, and valued.

THE THIRD STEP is to value his profession. I was at a church retreat once where a woman shared a song she wrote to esteem her husband. When she wrote it he was working in a hot dog stand, and she proudly called herself the woman lucky enough to have married the hot dog man. He was there when she shared the song, and he beamed with happiness. I don't know whatever became of the hot dog man and his wife, but I do know whatever that man chooses to do in his life he'll be successful. Not because of how much money he makes or how many degrees he may acquire but because he has a woman who believes in him. Make it a habit to praise your husband often. Let him hear you telling other people how proud you are to be married to such an amazing man. Watch out for things that may threaten him such as comparing him to other men or complaining constantly about his long hours.

THE LAST STEP is to ask God to make you sensitive to what your husband is facing. Ask for wisdom to know how to build him up. Pray that God would reveal to him how to keep his life in balance. Ask God to bless your husband with godly coworkers who can encourage him, for a close friend who can be an accountability partner, and an older man who can mentor him. Most of all pray that God would show you how to be the helpmate this precious husband of yours so desperately needs, one who offers help in a gentle understanding way, one who understands his fears, one who values his profession, and one who daily lifts him to new heights with her prayers.

RELATIONSHIP BUILDER—*Ask your husband today if he could do anything in the world and was sure not to fail, what would he do? Use what he tells you as a springboard for your prayers.*

THOUGHT FOR THE DAY—*Do you not know? Have you not heard? The LORD is the everlasting God, the Creator of the ends of the earth. He will not grow tired or weary, and his understanding no one can fathom. He gives strength to the weary and increases the power of the weak. Even youths grow tired and weary, and young men stumble and fall; but those who hope in the LORD will renew their strength. They will soar on wings like eagles; they will run and not grow weary, they will walk and not be faint.—[ISAIAH 40:28–31]*

CHAPTER 12

HOME: HAVEN OR HEADACHE?

I have to laugh when I see a clip from one of the old TV shows. Dad comes home from the office at 5:30 on the dot. Mom greets him wearing an apron, high heels, and lipstick. The oven bell rings one minute after she greets him with a peck on the cheek signaling that the perfectly cooked roast is done. The three happy, clean, adorably dressed children march downstairs in a single file line to greet Dad one by one and take their places at the dinner table. Dad takes off his suit jacket and neatly hangs it in the well-organized coat closet before joining his happy family at the table. They eat and lovingly converse. Then after dinner, Dad plays ball with Junior in the backyard while the two girls clean the kitchen and Mom fixes dessert. They all sit together on the back porch eating apple pie and talk about how swell their day has been.

The reason I laugh is because I assumed my home would be that inviting for my husband's arrival home from work. But between my bad attitude and my home's less-than-tidy atmosphere, my husband's welcome home was nothing like that. I'm not saying that the picture those shows painted was realistic but did I have to be at the opposite end of the spectrum? I suspected my attitude and my home's atmosphere had something to do with the difference.

First, my attitude. Let's play out this scene and see if we can identify with one of the reactions.

"Hi, honey, I'm home," he calls out after arriving an hour late.

OPTION ONE: "Where have you been? You were supposed to be home an hour ago. You know I am so sick and tired of you saying one thing and doing another. The phone company called; our payment is late again but what do you care? Between your cell phone, office phone, beeper, and fax, I bet you could care less if we had a phone at home. Did you ever consider that our home phone is my only lifeline to the real world. You try staying at home with small kids all day long and see if you wouldn't feel a little stressed if they threatened to take your phone away! Oh, and the kids and I already ate, so once again no quality time for the family. Boy, we feel real important. Do you keep us around just so you can have a token family picture to put on your desk at the office?"

OPTION TWO: "Hi, I'm in here. The kids and I have already eaten but would love to share a little dessert with you. Why don't you go put on some comfortable clothes, and I'll reheat your dinner. I bet you're exhausted from working overtime. After dessert, I have a couple things that we need to talk about."

I have reacted like option one more times than I care to admit. I know how it feels to be overwhelmed, stressed, and pushed to your limit. It's like you've been living for that minute that he walks in the door and offers some relief. When that minute comes an hour late, it's maddening! Unfortunately I also know the devastating results that come from my poorly chosen reaction. It has caused my husband to pull inside his shell and feel attacked and unappreciated.

When I have chosen the better reaction, option two, where he's greeted with grace and understanding, there's no place he'd rather be than home. I could blame my husband for being late and nag him, but will that get me the end result I so desire? No. What I want is a happy husband. I want him to be willing to pitch in and help. I want him to be excited about spending time with the kids and me. If I want him to enjoy our home, my attitude is key to making it happen. If there are issues that need to be addressed, discuss them after he's eaten and had time to unwind.

The second component is the atmosphere of my home. Our home should be the haven. A safe place. A refuge. How do we make our home a haven and not a headache? Every husband's definition of what a haven is will be different. My husband likes our home to look nice, smell nice, and sound nice. He loves to walk in the door without tripping over anything, smell a scented candle burning or dinner cooking, and hear classical music playing.

In my surveys, one man said, "I love to come home from work to a well-ordered house, a home that is a place of peace and not confusion: no piles of laundry on the bed, no dishes in the sink, no clutter on the furniture."

What is your husband's definition of a haven? Maybe he doesn't mind the clutter but wants a nice meal. Or maybe he could care less about the meal but would like the beds made and toys picked up. Only you can make your home beautiful and inviting for him.

The world would say, "What? Is she crazy? He walks in an hour late and I'm supposed to heat his dinner and tell him to put on comfortable clothes! I'm supposed to make our home a haven for him after all I've been through today?" Trust me on this one. When you bless your husband, you will receive a blessing yourself—if not from your husband, from the Lord. God will honor you for honoring your husband. Determine to honor the Lord by honoring your husband with both your attitude and created atmosphere, take it one day at a time, and start working toward making your home the place his heart longs for.

RELATIONSHIP BUILDER—*Ask your husband what his definition of a haven is and make a list of things you can do to make this a reality.*

THOUGHT FOR THE DAY—*When I have chosen the better reaction, where he's greeted with grace and understanding, there's no place he'd rather be than home.*

—*[LYSA TERKEURST]*

*Your husband
needs you to
engage him
intellectually.*

CHAPTER 13

HUSBANDS ARE HUNTERS,
NOT HINTERS

C ommunication is a funny beast. I didn't need another lesson on this but I recently got one anyway when we printed a banner promoting a Christmas Conference. The banner was supposed to say, "Proverbs 31 Ministries Presents . . . A Christmas to Remember Conference, Saturday, November 10." When we sent the text via e-mail to the printing company, we put the font name we wanted them to use for our logo in parentheses.

We were excited when our banner finally went up. It was two-sided, strategically placed on a busy road in the heart of town. Many people would see this banner and hopefully be drawn to register for our event. Our excitement took an unexpected twist when we drove by to admire our big promotion piece only to discover this is what it said, "Proverbs 31 Ministries (NUPTIAL) Presents . . . A Christmas to Remember Conference, Saturday, November 10." Yikes! Nuptial is the font we wanted them to use. Never did we think they would actually print the word *nuptial!*

We didn't know whether to laugh or cry. Sharon, my partner, quipped, "Well, maybe people will think it's a two-for-one deal . . . hear some great Christmas ideas and get married all in the same day." Another friend tried to console me by saying, "Well, at least you didn't request the font called *Wingdings!*"

We definitely need to communicate but how hard it is to tame this monster. I'm sure you've seen this firsthand in your marriage. In *Capture Her Heart,* the companion to this book, I tried to explain to men the often misunderstood part of a woman's language called, *hints.*

Hints is a way for a wife to tell her husband something without coming out and saying it. Why would she want to do that? Because if she comes right out and says it, it ruins the outcome she desires. For example if your wife says to you, "I'm a little stressed out about Thursday. I've got a doctor's appointment, and I can't find anyone to watch Suzie." You might react by suggesting a few people she should ask or by telling her to reschedule. But what she's hinting to you is, "Will you take a late lunch and watch Suzie for me while I go to the doctor on Thursday?" What she wants to know is, in a bind are you willing to go the extra mile for her?

She uses hints, because she wants it to be your idea. She's clueing you in on something that you could do that would mean a lot to her. If you don't understand her hint and don't offer to help her, the next time you're having a heated discussion she'll remind you of the time she asked you to watch Suzie for her and you said no. You won't have a clue as to what she's referring to. Thus a breakdown in communication and another argument where you are left scratching your head wondering why women are so complicated.[1]

Now do you know what I'm talking about? I've been a master at hints, and it's gotten me into trouble through the years. Actually, it's gotten my husband in quite a bit of trouble. Can you relate?

Here are a few comments from men who responded to my surveys:

"Just tell me what you are thinking."—SCOTT [SHEFFIELD]

"Please have the ladies understand that we cannot read their minds. We need clear instructions."—JEFFREY [KINGS MOUNTAIN]

"Draw me a map to your heart and pray for me that I will stop and read the map or ask for directions."—JIM [MADISON]

What I've come to realize is that husbands are hunters, not hinters. Men process things differently than women do. They hear a problem and instantly they hunt for a solution, shoot the idea our way, and check it off their list. They like quick, nonemotional solutions.

Women are all about emotion. Behind many of the requests we hint about, there are underlying requests being made such as, "Show me you care," "Show me I'm special," or "Show me that you think of me during your day." We see our requests as relationship-building opportunities. They see them as problems to be solved. So how do we resolve this communication dilemma?

Why not make your daily requests plain and simple enough for him to understand and help him find creative ways to meet your underlying emotional needs? Every Sunday my husband and I have a meeting where we talk about our schedules for the week. I've learned to put hinting aside during these meetings and make my requests directly. I used to worry that I might be asking too much for him to take time after work to run an errand or pick up the kids from an extra-curricular activity—but not anymore. I'm not superwoman, and I can't do everything myself. He doesn't mind helping as long as I don't throw things at him at the last minute. If he has time to process my requests and there is no conflict with his schedule, he's usually more than willing to help.

About the underlying emotional needs, here's something to try. It's called "Love Jars." Get two empty jars and write your name on one and your husband's on the other. Put five slips of paper in both jars and ask your husband for time to do this exciting activity. When you both have time to sit down together, ask him to write down five things (one on each slip of paper) that would speak love in a way that would be especially meaningful to him. You do the same. Fold the notes in half and each of you tuck them away in your own jar. Each Sunday for the next five weeks, each of you picks from the other's jar one activity to do during that week. Keep it a secret and make sure to commit to doing for each other what the slip of paper you've chosen says. This is a lot of fun and will add a spark of excitement that can keep those home fires burning—to say nothing of what it will do to improve communication skills of the hunter and the hinter.

RELATIONSHIP BUILDER—*Gather the materials to put together his and hers "Love Jars." Plan to start the "Love Jar" activity this upcoming Sunday.*

 THOUGHT FOR THE DAY—*Draw me a map to your heart and pray for me that I will stop and read the map or ask for directions.—JIM [MADISON]*

CHAPTER 14

DANGERS OF THE LEAKY FAUCET

I didn't think the dripping was that big a deal. What harm can a little water do? I cleaned up the water that had been dripping from the pipe's seam near the floor and forgot about it. Several days later I noticed the floor was wet again. So, I cleaned it up and went on my way. I finally clued in that this might be a problem when I noticed the floor around the base of the sink was becoming damaged. I brought it to the attention of my husband, and he immediately shut the water supply off to the sink and called the plumber. We indeed had problems.

Many months later I came across verses in Proverbs that took on new meaning because of this whole leaky faucet situation. When I recorded these verses in my journal, I called them my "ouchie" marriage verses. I think you'll see why.

■ Proverbs 19:13: "A quarrelsome wife is like a constant dripping."

■ Proverbs 21:9: "Better to live on a corner of the roof than share a house with a quarrelsome wife."

■ Proverbs 21:19: "Better to live in a desert than with a quarrelsome and ill-tempered wife."

See what I mean? Ouch! The whole leaking sink situation

shed such light on a grave mistake I was making in my marriage. I realized I was a constant dripping in my husband's life. Instead of engaging him intellectually, I was engaging him in emotional battles he was ill-equipped to fight. I interpreted his actions and statements so much more emotionally than he ever intended them.

For example, once he called and offered to bring me lunch. I told him I wanted a grilled chicken sandwich and a Coke. I kept thinking this was such a sweet gesture of love and kindness. When he brought me my lunch, my grateful mood turned somber when I saw the diet button depressed on the top of my drink. To him it was a simple mistake. To me he was saying, "You're fat and ugly. You need to be drinking a diet drink so I changed your order." I was so hurt and angry. I "dripped" over this silly misunderstanding for days.

Each time I started dripping, Art was trying to quickly clean up the mess. But the dripping continued and he was getting weary with the constant return of the puddles. Finally, he started to shut down and tried to turn off the water supply. He felt he couldn't say anything right, so the safest thing to do would be to not talk at all. The water was eroding the foundation of our marriage. Time to call the plumber. We indeed had problems.

At the root of our issues was my inability to communicate without my feelings getting hurt. I felt I was not acceptable, beautiful, or capable of being loved. These wrong perceptions festered and ate away at the foundation of our marriage. They were like a filter over my mind that tainted, skewed, and misinterpreted comments my husband made. Could you possibly have this same kind of filter?

Satan was a master at helping me negate my self-worth by reminding me of painful things from my past. I thought getting married would fix a lot of these problems from my broken past. Now, I realized this filter was hurting not only me but my husband as well.

Slowly, God is replacing my filter of lies with His healing and transforming truth. God says in His Word that I'm a holy and dearly loved child of God. That's the filter my thoughts must pass through. Romans 12:2 says, "Do not conform any longer to the pattern of this world, but be transformed by the renewing of your mind. Then you will be able to test and approve what God's will is—his good, pleasing and perfect will." Conforming to the world means to act and react based on feelings. God wants to transform our minds so we act and react based on His truths not our feelings.

The truth is that my husband loves me and is committed to our relationship. The truth is that he thinks I'm beautiful and fun to be with. The truth is that he loves honoring God by honoring me. The truth is that he sometimes makes mistakes in the way he phrases things or in a careless action, but it does not mean he doesn't love me. Most importantly God loves me and God loves my husband and bestows so much grace and forgiveness on us, how could we ever dare not to extend them to each other?

If you sense your faucet has been a little leaky lately, here are some ways to get past being your husband's complainer and into being his beloved companion:

■ Let God's Word be your constant reminder of your worth and significance.

■ If your husband says something that hurts your feelings, give him the benefit of the doubt before getting upset.

■ Ask him to clarify what he meant by what he said.

■ If what he said is hurtful, calmly explain why his statement hurt you and suggest a better way for him to communicate the point he's trying to make next time.

■ Be willing to err on the side of grace.

■ Be quick to forgive.

■ Pick your battles wisely. Some things aren't worth getting upset over.

■ Be willing to let the little things slide.

■ Try to be the first to say you're sorry.

RELATIONSHIP BUILDER—*Think about what you might do to repair any leaks that may have sprung up lately from your faucet. Write out the suggestions above in first person and stick them in your Bible. The next time you spring a leak, get your list and make repairs quickly.*

 THOUGHT FOR THE DAY—*Better to live in a desert than with a quarrelsome and ill-tempered wife.*
—*[PROVERBS 21:19]*

CHAPTER 15

THE POWER OF THE SHARED DREAM

I love talking to people on airplanes. I always feel as though God has divine appointments with whomever He sits me beside, and today is no exception. I am flying back from a retreat in Alaska. I just finished an encouraging talk with the man seated beside me. He told me he and his wife had been married for thirty-one years and that he was still madly in love with her. I told him I was writing a book on marriage and would love his perspective on what helped him and his wife stay together and stay in love for all those years. He told me it's not complicated. He respected her and she respected him. He did what he could to make her happy, and she did the same.

I asked him what had kept the passion in their relationship. He told me about the dream they shared their whole married life. For thirty-one years they had a common goal to save enough money to buy a horse ranch. Neither of them had great-paying jobs but they lived within their means and saved faithfully. Last year they retired and bought their ranch. He said they've never had so much fun in all their life, and the bond between them keeps growing stronger every day.

Contrast that with another conversation I had recently. It was with a wife of another man. They'd been married for close to twenty years. It was obvious from the way she talked that her marriage lacked in the passion department. The every-

84

dayness of life had taken a toll on their relationship. They lived above their means and barely scraped by paycheck to paycheck. They had a lot of things but were unhappy. They never shared a common dream and now weren't even sure if they wanted a future together. They had no common goals. No common dreams. Maybe not even a common future.

Sometimes the only thing that gets us through today is the hope tomorrow holds. When your tomorrows start seeming less hopeful, the problems of today consume and destroy a person and a relationship. Have you and your husband spent time talking about your future? Do you have common goals that you are working toward together? Do you have any idea what dreams might be tucked in your husband's heart? Does he have any idea of your dreams?

 My mother-in-law and I were talking this morning about how amazing it is that in ten years God has not only turned my marriage around but now has Art and me writing and speaking to help other couples. If God could do this for us, He could do this for you. Art says,

All husbands have dreams—whether they are career-centered or family-centered. If a wife can get her husband to share those dreams and help him fulfill those dreams, it would help him have a passion to help her realize her dreams. Couples should have shared dreams where they have common goals and aspirations for their future together.

I did a devotional the other day that explained what fertilizer does for a plant, pursuing God's purpose does for a life. Dreaming God's divine plan and purpose for your life and your marriage will cause growth. When a wife taps into this growth potential, wonderful things are bound to happen.

Anytime you approach someone from their vantage point and draw out of them their passions and dreams, people light up. What would happen if you went to your husband and asked him what his dreams are and what you could do to help him fulfill them? If you follow through with the commitments you make to him, you'll see a changed man and one who is suddenly passionate about his helpmate.

I can't say I've done this perfectly. I did a poor job of even knowing what Art's dreams were in the beginning. It has been a process, but one well worth the effort. There is something magical about dreaming together. There is something passionate about working together to unlock those dreams and turn them into reality. I like the way Robert Lewis and William Hendricks explain it:

A wise woman . . . is patient with her husband during dream sessions. She understands that after three or four weeks of getting pushed around at his job, it's only natural for him to start dreaming about becoming a professional mountain climber or joining the circus or some other crazy scheme. She also realizes that dreaming is his way of evaluating. Often he's really asking: Is what I'm doing *valuable?* Am I any good? Does my life count for anything? Is there anything else I could do? What do you think of me? (P.S.: I'm feeling insecure!) Questions like these are the very reason you as a wife need to be there, sharing his dreams.—*[Robert Lewis and William Hendricks]*[1]

Relationship Builder—*Have a dream conversation with your husband this week. Make some notes on things that you could do to help him.*

 Thought for the Day—*A wise woman . . . is patient with her husband during dream sessions. . . . Often he's really asking: Is what I'm doing* valuable? *Am I any good? Does my life count for anything? Is there anything else I could do? What do you think of me?—[Robert Lewis and William Hendricks]*[2]

Your husband needs you to connect with him relationally.

CHAPTER 16

DISCOVERING WHAT MAKES HIM TICK
WTHOUT TICKING HIM OFF

Years ago I was listening to a presentation by Zig Zigler where he asked us to play a game I want to do with you. Are you one of the zillions of people who faithfully strap a timepiece to your wrist every day? If not, bear with me here. If so, don't look at your watch! Not even a little peek. Without looking, tell me what kinds of numerals does it have . . . roman numerals, standard numbers, dots, dashes, nothing at all? What is at the 12:00 spot, the 3:00 spot, the 6:00 spot, and the 9:00 spot? Now check your watch. Examine it closely. Are you surprised? How many answers did you get correct? Now, since you've just examined your watch. Without looking again, what time is it?

Think of how many times a day you look at your watch, and yet many of us can't recall the simplest of details about it. Too many of our marriages are the same way. The extraordinary flame between newlyweds seems to slow to a small flicker and husbands and wives are left scratching their heads wondering what went wrong.

When we are dating one thing that makes us so exciting to each other is the new discoveries about each other that we spend time unearthing. We dig into one another's childhood, high school and college experiences, family life, holiday traditions, and aspirations for the future. We take time to share the details of our experiences, our thoughts, our hopes, and even our fears. While listening we take mental notes and become students of one another looking for ways to build new experiences that become "we/us" shared memories. All the newness is exhilarating and serves to stoke the flames of romance. Then you get married and have a couple of children and suddenly every conversation becomes Cliff notes versions. There's no time for in-depth reviews and new discoveries; there are diapers to change and bills to pay and things to acquire.

So we slip into survival mode and stop discovering all together. Think back to our watch illustration. I wonder how many things there are that we have no clue about where our husbands are concerned? I look at him every day, sleep with him at night, talk, kiss, and even make babies with him yet there's still much I don't know. And sadly, much of what I do know and love has gotten lost in the shuffle of life. It helps to think back to those dating days and resurrect the desire to discover what makes him tick a priority.

Here are some ideas of questions to ask to help get you started:

■ What is your favorite color?

■ What does your ideal Christmas look like?

■ When do I look most attractive to you?

■ Is there anything that you've been wanting to share with me but haven't for fear of offending me? I'll give you the chance and promise not to get emotional about your answer.

■ What is an ideal gift to you?

■ If you could start all over again after high school, what are some things you would do differently?

■ If you could only give our children three pieces of advice, what would they be and why?

■ If you had to write one sentence to be put on your tombstone, what would you like it to say?

■ If you could be known as an expert of one thing, what would that be and why?

■ What is your favorite game?

■ What makes you feel relaxed and comfortable enough to unwind?

■ What is your favorite Bible verse?

■ Define romance.

■ In your opinion, what is the most romantic thing we've ever done?

■ How can I be a better friend to you?

■ What is something you've always wanted to do but haven't because of financial limitations?

This is just a start. This is not a checklist for you to sit down and run through. These questions are simply conversation starters to get creative juices flowing in your marriage. If we are ever going to connect with our husbands relationally, we've got to enter into their worlds and discover what they are thinking and dreaming about. Determine to become a life-long student of your mate. The more you discover about what makes him tick, the less likely you are to tick him off, and I think we're all for that. Then, much like that old Timex commercial, our relationships will be able to, "take a licking and keep on ticking!"

RELATIONSHIP BUILDER—*Start a "My Marriage Is Incredible!" journal. It can be a little spiral notebook or a decorative journal. Learn two new things about your husband today and record them in your journal. Make it a habit to record good marriage Bible verses you come across and quotes you find inspiring. Record marriage lessons you read about or experience. Praise God for all He teaches you about loving your husband and giving yourself to another person.*

 THOUGHT FOR THE DAY—*If anything is excellent or praiseworthy—think about such things.—[PHILIPPIANS 4:8]*

CHAPTER 17

UNDERSTANDING HIS
COMPARTMENT DEPARTMENT

This is not going to come as a news flash, but it is worth discussing . . . men think differently than women. When I asked Sherry, who works in our office, what she thought women could benefit from understanding about their husbands, she was quick to say, "One thing I've learned about men, they do not like to do more than one thing at a time. Women like to multitask, men do not." Well said. Men like to focus on one thing at a time. Women can do many things at once and really enjoy doing them. I can put on my makeup, talk on the phone, scold my children, and listen to the radio all while driving down the highway . . . and they say women can't drive.

My husband, on the other hand, likes to watch football or check his stocks on the computer or talk on the phone or talk to me—one at a time. Throw all those things at him at once and several things get tuned out while he focuses on one. In conversations with my husband, if I try to bounce from subject to subject, he gets equally confused. He tries to focus on one aspect of our conversation and bring that one to a close before moving on to another. Meanwhile, I'm all over the place and I get frustrated when I see the glazed look in his eyes that tells me he appears to be tuning me out.

Before I understood that my husband's brain is divided into compartments, we had many conversations that went something like this:

Lysa: Hi, honey, how was your day?

Art: Good.

Lysa: Mine too. I took Hope and Ashley for their well checkups today. (Meaning I took the girls to the doctor not because they were sick but because it was time for their annual physicals.)

Art: (Silently wondering what our water well needed to be checked for and how our daughters fit into the same sentence.)

Lysa: (Feeling a little frustrated at his silence, which I interpret as a lack of caring.) And, they were fine . . . (thinking: *Not that you seem to care.*)

Art: (Still silently wondering what our well water needed to be checked for and how our daughters fit into it.)

Lysa: Anyhow, (obviously annoyed), on my way to the doctor's office I was driving down Providence Road, and I noticed all the trees had black tape wrapped around them. It appears to be some sort of pest control treatment. Do you think our trees could be in danger of these bugs? Because if so, I think

I'd like to try this tape stuff, which is probably a lot safer than spraying chemicals that could harm the children. You know I just don't think our government is doing enough to protect our kids from dangerous pesticides. So, do you think I should spend extra money at the grocery store for organic produce? If so, I'll need you to add some money to my grocery budget.

Art: (Wondering how the well, our daughters, the trees on Providence Road, and the government's stand on pesticides could end in a request to spend more money. He decides to play it safe.) I don't know, honey; I'll have to think about it.

Lysa: (Astonished at his lack of concern for our family's health begins to cry.) You'll have to think about what? We are talking about our daughters' lives here and all you can say is you'll think about it!

Art: (Baffled, still not understanding how any of this relates to our daughters' lives but clearly understanding I'm asking for more money again.) Why are you so emotional, and why are you always nagging me for more money? (He realizes he shouldn't have said *nagging*, remembering he got something thrown at him the last time he used that word. He regrets his choice of words and ducks just in case.)

Lysa: Nagging? You call caring for our children, *nagging?* You are so insensitive . . . you're impossible. You're not worth wasting any more of my breath! (Stomp, stomp, stomp, slam.)

Art: *Women! What's the deal? And what did she ever say was wrong with our well?*

How complicated we can make the simplest conversations. We can blow the smallest issues out of proportion. A simple clarification and an understanding of how our minds process information differently could have circumvented many arguments in my marriage.

In recent years, several books have been written to help bridge the gap between the different genders. One by Bill and Pam Farrel is titled, *Men Are Like Waffles, Women Are Like Spaghetti.* In their hilariously insightful explanation of the book's title, they explain men and women in these terms:

Men Are Like Waffles: "We do not mean that men 'waffle' on all decisions and are generally unstable. What we mean is that men process life in boxes. If you look down at a waffle, you see a collection of boxes separated by walls. The boxes are all separate from each other and make convenient holding places. That is typically how a man processes life. Our thinking is divided up into boxes that have room for one issue and one issue only."[1] They continue that men organize every category of their life in separate boxes and like to spend time in the boxes they can succeed in. They have boxes where there are nice thoughts and memories, and other boxes that are blank that have no thoughts or words—thus their ability to tune out at times.

But *Women Are Like Spaghetti:* "In contrast to men's waffle approach, women process life like a plate of pasta. If you look at a plate of spaghetti, you notice that there are lots of individual noodles that all touch one another. If you attempted to follow one noodle around the plate, you would intersect a lot of other noodles, and you might even switch to another noodle seamlessly. This is how women face life. Every thought and issue is connected to every other thought and issue in some way. Life is much more of a process for women than for men."[2]

What a great description. By realizing the compartmentalized approach men take when processing information and conversing with us, we can better understand how to help them stay tuned in. My new rule I try to remember when having a discussion with my man is "one thing at a time, and clarify, clarify, clarify!"

RELATIONSHIP BUILDER—*Discuss with your husband the waffle/ spaghetti idea. Strategize some ways the two of you can more effectively communicate. Maybe you'll even want to check out Bill and Pam Farrel's book for a more in-depth study of this concept.*

 THOUGHT FOR THE DAY—*Men typically organize every category of their life in separate boxes and like to spend time in the boxes that they can succeed in.*

—*[BILL AND PAM FARREL]*

CHAPTER 18

THE KEY TO BECOMING YOUR HUSBAND'S FRIEND . . . LAUGHTER!

A rt and I enjoy teaching classes together at our church. Art is the organized one who makes sure all the i's are dotted and the t's are crossed. I'm the entertaining one who makes sure our classes are fun. You never know what might happen when I step up to the podium.

One night we were teaching on spiritual gifts. He would teach for twenty minutes and then I would teach for twenty minutes and then we'd switch. I'd just started teaching one of my sections when out of the corner of my eye I saw Art writing a note. I knew the note was addressed to me because I could see my name at the top. Then I caught a glimpse of the end of the note, which read, "I love you that much. . . . Art."

My heart swelled with excitement. My husband was writing me a love note, right in the middle of our class! I became extra animated in my instructing. I was absolutely giddy with thoughts like: *He thinks I'm pretty. He's just captivated by my beauty! He is so in love with me. I'm the luckiest woman alive!*

Finally, I couldn't stand it any longer. I had to read the note. I gave the class a long verse to write out, which afforded me time to get the note and indulge.

"Dear Lysa, You have a booger in your left nose. I'll get it for you if you like. I love you that much, Art."

Mortified does not even begin to describe what I felt. I quickly finished my section hiding my nose as much as possible and excused myself to the bathroom. What I discovered in the bathroom was no small flake. Cliff-hanger is the only word to describe what I found. If someone could die from embarrassment, I almost did.

Sheepishly, I made my way back to the class. Suddenly, a hilarious thought struck me. As I took my place back up front with Art, I grabbed the note and wrote on the bottom, "YOU DO TOO!"

Poor Art, he got wide-eyed and barely made it through his teaching session for all his sniffing and attempts to hide his nose. He, of course, had nothing out of normal about his nose, but I just had to let him share in all the excitement.

On our way home that night, we laughed hysterically about all that had happened. Somewhere in all the laughter the thought struck me that we had become best friends. Who else but your best friend says, "I'll get it for you if you like . . . I love you that much."

Somehow through all the ups and downs we have found this precious and rare facet to our relationship—the ability to be friends and laugh with each other. Proverbs 17:22 says, "A cheerful heart is good medicine." How true!

"Humor can be developed, and should be, because it contributes to good health. Laughter's known benefits include:

■ It stimulates the immune system.

■ It pulls together various parts of the brain rather than activating a component in only one area. Perhaps this is one reason people often find that a dose of lengthy laughter can be followed by a burst of creativity and problem solving.

■ It's a good cardio-thoracic workout. It increases the activity of the heart and stimulates circulation. After laughter subsides, the cardiovascular system goes into a state of relaxation.

■ It raises the threshold of pain. It has been shown that five minutes of giggling may provide up to two hours of pain relief.

■ It reduces stress.

■ It stabilizes moods.

■ It rests the brain.

■ It enhances communication."[1]

Many times in my marriage I have not responded to situations in laughter but rather in bitterness and resentment. Reacting out of anger never leads anywhere positive. I've learned over the years the importance of making choices that lead to good outcomes rather than simply reacting to circumstances. Learning to laugh with Art is the key that has opened the door of friendship for us.

Let me encourage you to learn to laugh with your husband. Make the conscious decision the next time you feel tension rising over a situation to diffuse it with a kind or funny word. Proverbs 12:25 says, "An anxious heart weighs a man down, but a kind word cheers him up."

Think about a cheerleader on the sidelines of a game. What do they say when their team has messed up? "That's all right, that's OK. We're gonna beat 'em anyway." Wouldn't it be great to be that kind of cheerleader for our husbands when tense situations arise? Choosing to be kind, encouraging, or even humorous is not the easiest response but it is the best. If I can find humor in my cliff-hanger, I'm convinced there is laughter to be found in any situation.

RELATIONSHIP BUILDER—*Ask your husband if the two of you can share your most embarrassing moments. Read him mine if you like, and the two of you can laugh together.*

 THOUGHT FOR THE DAY—*There is a time for everything, and a season for every activity under heaven . . . a time to weep and a time to laugh.*—[ECCLESIASTES 3:1, 4]

Your husband

needs you to

affirm him

physically.

CHAPTER 19

GOD DESIGNED US PHYSICALLY DIFFERENT

During one of my trips to the bookstore to do research, I came across a book written by a man that promised new ideas to "woo and wow the one you love." I was intrigued, so I flipped through the pages and read some of his ideas. Suddenly, I burst out laughing uncontrollably as I read this idea for a romantic date, "You can even make cleaning the bathroom romantic, if you're clever about it! Here's how one couple does it: 1) They clean the bathroom together, 2) They time themselves to see how quickly they can do it, and 3) They do it in the nude. (What???) As you can imagine, they're always bumping into each other, they're hurrying and laughing and making a scene." He goes on to suggest, "And then there's nude dusting, nude room painting, nude dish washing . . ."[1] Just the thought of this cracks me up! This book was definitely written by a man.

It reminds me of two magazine ads Art and I use when teaching our marriage seminars. The first is a shoe ad that goes along the theme of the bathroom date idea. It features a woman dressed in a pink slip, full makeup and styled hair, wearing high heels while cleaning a toilet. She has a seductive look on her face and seems to find something romantic about this less than fun household chore. Not one woman I've ever met feels that sexy while cleaning toilets. But, this is a husband's dream wife: meeting all his needs at once. Just give her a toilet brush and suddenly while cleaning she's transformed into a sex goddess.

Contrast that with ad number two. It's for a Lane Cedar Chest. It features a happy couple in a sweet embrace with words written below them that say something to this effect, "My wife saves everything I ever give her. From the box that the ring was in to our anniversary cards. Now she'll have a place to put it all—a Lane Cedar Chest." Talk about romance! Talk about thoughtfulness. My heart goes pitter-patter every time I read that ad. Art rolls his eyes and tries to assure me the first ad is much more appealing. Oh, how different we are.

 Not only do we know about this difference from our everyday experiences, but research proves it. Here are some facts that studies have found about the differences between men and women:

■ Before we are born, differences in the sexes can be found. Dr. Frank Duffy recorded the brain activity of boys and girls still in the womb and found they were on two different wavelengths.[2]

■ Medical studies have reported that during the eighteenth and twenty-sixth week of pregnancy brain damage occurs to little boy fetuses that forever separate the sexes. Sex-related hormones flood a boy baby's brain causing the right side to recede slightly, destroying some of the connecting fibers. As a result, in most cases, a boy starts life more left-brain oriented. (The left brain houses more of the logical, analytical, factual, and aggressive centers of thought.)[3]

■ From birth, girls have more lip movement than boys.[4]

■ As we move into the preschool years, nearly 100 percent of the sounds that come from little girls' mouths are audible recognizable words. For boys only 68 percent of their sounds tend to be recognizable words while the other 32 percent are one-syllable sounds.[5]

■ As we mature, it has been shown that the average male speaks about 12,500 words a day while the average female speaks 25,000![6]

God designed us to be different so that when we come together, we build a beautiful God-glorifying one. It's not coming together to see which one is the right one and which one is wrong and then weeding out the "wronger" of the two. No, it's you building and investing your strengths to help your husband become all God intended him to be and it's him doing the same for you. When this works, it is a beautiful picture of affirmation physically, sexually, emotionally, and spiritually.

We've covered the sexual, emotional, and spiritual aspects of affirmation in other chapters so let me leave you with a story of physical affirmation that I hope will inspire you. It's the story of Peter Foster, a Royal Air Force pilot in World

War II. "During an air battle, Foster was a victim of a terrible fire. He survived, but his face was burned beyond recognition. He spent many anxious moments in the hospital wondering if his family—and especially his fiancée—would still accept him. They did. His fiancée assured him that nothing had changed except a few millimeters of skin. Two years later they were married. Foster said of his wife, 'She became my mirror. She gave me a new image of myself. When I look at her, she gives me a warm, loving smile that tells me I'm okay.'"[7]

This story is in Dr. James and Shirley Dobson's couple's devotional, *Night Light*. They comment about this story, saying, "That's the way marriage ought to work, too—it should be a mutual admiration society that overlooks a million flaws and builds the self-esteem of both partners."[8]

What a great example of getting past differing and getting on with making a difference in one another's life. God made us different—not to hinder one another but to help.

RELATIONSHIP BUILDING—*Make a list of strengths your husband has and write him a thank-you letter for all the good he's added to your life.*

 THOUGHT FOR THE DAY—*Let your conversation be always full of grace.*—[COLOSSIANS 4:6]

CHAPTER 20

LOVING THE LOVE HANDLES

First of all I must tell you that my husband is one of the most physically fit people I've ever met. If anyone is going to struggle with having love handles, it will be I. Actually, not love handles but saddlebags. While Art is physically fit, he does have areas where he wants and needs my affirmation. The point is that we all have things about ourselves that we don't like. Places where insecurity trips us up. Next to the Lord, our spouse's unconditional love can and should be of great comfort to us.

We see our husbands exposed for who they are, and they want to know that we accept them. Men put on good acts in public. Most appear tough and secure and sure of themselves. They are called on to be leaders, protectors, and decision makers. Deep inside, though, rivers of doubt and uncertainty flow. They need their wives to affirm them—to tell them that they love them no matter what.

A good example of this "no matter what love" is found in the story of Dave Dravecky (a professional baseball player) and his wife, Jan. In *When You Can't Come Back* they chronicle the events and the emotions of Dave's bout with cancer, amazing comeback, and devastating amputation of his award-winning pitching arm.

When Dave was a boy, his world revolved around baseball.

When he got older and discovered he was a talented pitcher, his identity centered around his arm. He said, "My arm was to me what hands are to a concert pianist, what legs are to a ballerina, what feet are to a marathon runner. . . . It's what made me valuable, what gave me worth, at least in the eyes of the world. Then suddenly my arm was gone. How much of me went with it? How much of what people thought of me went with it?"

He goes on to say about Jan, "How would my wife feel? What would she think about a man who couldn't tie his own shoes? Would she still find me attractive, or would she be repulsed to see me in my nakedness with my carved-up body? When I came home from the hospital, I realized . . . all Jan wanted was to have her husband back."

 He concluded by saying, "As important as it had been to my boyhood, as important as it had been to my livelihood, my arm meant nothing to the people in my life who mattered most. It was enough that I was alive and that I was home."[1]

Remember the vows most of us naively repeated, "in good times and bad, in sickness and health." To love unconditionally means to let our husbands know in word and deed that we will be by their side if they make a fortune or fall flat on their faces in business. We'll be there if they are strong and able, and we'll still be there if they get sick or crippled. They have a lifelong partner whether they are fit and lean, or wrinkly, gray, and saggy. Just like that old Band-aid commercial, our husbands need to know we are stuck on them.

For a more personal story, here's a note from Art:

I've always tried hard to wisely save and invest our family's money. It's important for me to provide our monthly needs and to look ahead at our financial future. Maybe part of my significance was wrapped up in my financial abilities. I knew everything came from God, and I was diligent about not only saving but tithing as well. Then one day, my carefully constructed investing plan came crashing down as one of my investments went bad. I must say it rocked me to my core.

I couldn't understand why God allowed us to lose so much when we were trying to be faithful stewards of what He'd entrusted to us. I felt sick, my spirit was crushed, and my confidence sank to an all-time low. I expected Lysa to feel as devastated as I was, which would have made me feel even worse. Instead when I told her about the magnitude of the situation, she wrapped her arms around me and said everything was going to be fine. It's amazing how her words of comfort became a wellspring for me to release all the hurt and anguish I was feeling.

I know that a husband's provision of security is one of a woman's greatest needs. Lysa's unconditional love in an area where she is most vulnerable was an amazing form of healing for me. Had she reacted the way I expected, I would have continued to focus on the problem and its solution. Instead she gave me a license to heal and allowed me to focus on God's direction and His promise to take care of us. Then she said something I'll never forget. She said, "Art, I love you for who you are, not for what you have." I can't tell you how much her unconditional love at that point meant to me.

Rest assured, wives, there have been many times where I've blown it, but thankfully I chose a good response in that situation. Habakkuk 3:17–19 says, "Though the fig tree does not bud and there are no grapes on the vines, though the olive crop fails and the fields produce no food, though there are no sheep in the pen and no cattle in the stalls, yet I will rejoice in the LORD, I will be joyful in God my Savior. The Sovereign LORD is my strength; he makes my feet like the feet of a deer, he enables me to go on the heights." If you might allow me to use this as my inspiration and write a Habakkuk 3 for marriage:

Though he may have gained a little weight and lost a little hair, though the castle I always dreamed of is only a three-bedroom ranch, though there are no maids in the servant quarters and nothing but a beat-up old minivan in the driveway, yet I will rejoice in the husband the Lord has blessed me with, I will be joyful in being this man's wife. The Sovereign Lord is my strength; He helps me have a good attitude even during PMS, He lifts me from my many loads of laundry and helps me to see the eternal significance of being my husband's lover, helper, and friend.

RELATIONSHIP BUILDER—*Write the words, "I love you just because you are you—forever and ever," on little slips of paper and hide them in places your husband is sure to find them. Look for opportunities to reassure him of your love on a daily basis.*

THOUGHT FOR THE DAY—*Be completely humble and gentle; be patient, bearing with one another in love.* —[EPHESIANS 4:2]

CHAPTER 21

BECOMING HIS BEAUTY

Ponytail holders. Pink bows and ribbons. Lace tablecloths. Spring scented candles. Bubble baths. Night cream, eye cream, foundation, cover-up, mascara, lip liner, eyeliner, lipstick, gloss, eye shadow, and blush. Posies and pansies and daffodils and daisies. Teacups and sugar cubes. Chocolate, chocolate, and more chocolate with chocolate syrup on top. Giggles and girl talk.

I think I've succeeded in scaring any husbands out of this chapter if they happened to be thumbing through your book to see what it says. This is our secret chapter. The information here is for feminine eyes only. The information here could have you and your girlfriends gabbing for days! I'm simply reporting to the facts that I've discovered. So without further ado . . . here goes.

How do you become the beauty your husband wants to capture and never let go? How do you get him to be the man . . . the romantic man of your dreams? How do you get him thinking of you and wanting to do romantic things for you? How do you get your warrior to fight for you because you're beautiful and he can't imagine a day without you? How do you get him to fix that leaking toilet and take out the trash without being asked? How do you get him to pitch in and help with the kids and around the house? How do you get him to pay more attention to you than to his work or sports or hunting?

You seduce him.

Ohmygoodness! (That's a southern expression I picked up from a dear friend of mine named Dolly and the only one appropriate after a sentence like that!)

I said it. Yes, Christian sisters of mine, you seduce him!

John Eldridge in his book, *Wild at Heart,* says, "I'm telling you that the church has really crippled women when it tells them that their beauty is vain and they are at their feminine best when they are 'serving others.' A woman is at her best when she is being a woman." He goes on to say that if a woman wants her man to do something, she has several options. "She can badger him: *All you ever do is work, work, work. Why don't you stand up and be a man?* She can whine about it and in essence emasculate him: *I thought you were a real man; I guess I was wrong.* Or she can use all she is as a woman to get him to use all he's got as a man. She can arouse, inspire, energize . . . seduce him. Ask your man which he'd prefer."[1]

I love that line, "use all she is as a woman to get him to use all he's got as a man." That's what it means to become his beauty. I can tell you're thinking, *We've already covered this sex stuff—why are we revisiting this topic?* This seduction is more than a sexual thing. It is about becoming the beauty that draws the heart of your man into the oneness God intended for the two of you to have. A man's heart is drawn out by a woman's beauty. The deep parts of him suddenly expose themselves when he's made to feel desired and attracted.

It is hard for a woman to desire to attract her husband if she herself does not feel attractive. Patrick Morley in his book,

What Husbands Wish Their Wives Knew About Men, says, "A typical husband wants his wife to look good, but he is not obsessed. However, he does consider his wife's appearance a reflection on his judgment. A man wants to feel proud of his wife. What a man hopes for is that his wife will portray a certain dignity in her looks that is consistent with his image of himself." He goes on to say, "If any wife reading this book could say, 'If my husband died, after my mourning time I would lose thirty pounds, fix my hair a new way, and buy a new wardrobe,' she can be almost certain of this: Her husband secretly wishes she would go ahead and do it now."[2]

 A woman's inner spirit also needs to be attractive to her husband. First Peter 3:3–6 explains that for a woman to be truly beautiful she must have the "unfading beauty of a gentle and quiet spirit." This does not mean she is to be quiet all the time but rather exude a spirit of loveliness that her husband wants to be around. It is God's design that a woman—someone so completely feminine and intoxicating to him—helps him let his guard down and makes him feel free to let masculinity surge through him. She's fully feminine and he's fully masculine, and the two make a beautiful one.

The beauty needs her man. The man needs his beauty. God designed for this oneness to delight us, energize us, and fulfill our longings to be desired. First Corinthians 7:3–5 says, "The man should give his wife all that is her right as a married woman, and the wife should do the same for her husband; for a girl who marries no longer has full right to her own body, for her husband then has his rights to it too; and in the same way the husband no longer has full right to his own body for it belongs also to his wife. So do not refuse these rights to each other. The only exception to this rule would be the agreement of both husband and wife to refrain from the rights of marriage for a limited time, so that they can give themselves more completely to prayer. Afterwards, they should come together again so that Satan won't be able to tempt them because of their lack of self-control" (TLB).

Author Chuck Snyder in his book, *Men: Some Assembly Required,* says, "It's interesting to look up the Greek meaning of 'come together again' in the above passage. The Greek word is *hupotasso-whoopee!* meaning three or more times a week. Now, don't blame me ladies. Look up the Greek for yourself."[3]

Maybe that's where we got the expression, "Let's make whoopee!" Do you want to become the beauty in the romance God is writing between you and your husband? I know I do. So let's make it a practice to become the beauty, inside and out, who isn't afraid to seduce and make some *hupotasso-whoopee!*

RELATIONSHIP BUILDER—*I think I'll let you get creative and write your own assignment for today.*

 THOUGHT FOR THE DAY—*Hupotasso-whoopee. Enough said.*

*Your husband
needs you to
stand by him
permanently.*

CHAPTER 22

FOR BETTER OR WORSE

I am so glad I stuck it out," the fun-loving lady said as she told me how she was crazy in love with her husband. She went on, "Ten years ago I was ready to call it quits. He was so inconsiderate and had put me through so much. Not a day went by that he didn't do something that hurt me. Sometimes they were small things and other days they were really hurtful things, but all added together they made me miserable. I would think, *This is not what I bargained for—this is not how things should be!* I had always dreamed of a fairytale marriage, but not one where the prince turned into a frog. My storybooks always had it the other way around!"

I felt compelled to ask her how things improved so dramatically that she now is eager to tell others she is crazy about her husband. "It wasn't easy," she was quick to answer, "but I prayed that God would honor my decision to honor my commitment. The more I focused on God and not my marriage, the more God filled in the gaps. God carried me through and helped me. He encouraged me when I felt discouraged. He strengthened me when I felt weak and weary. He helped me love my husband even though I did not feel like it. Over time I witnessed a miracle take place in my husband. God changed him, softened him, and revealed to him the way he should treat me. I can honestly say I can't imagine what my life would be like if I'd given up. I've finally found that fairytale."

Her words encouraged me because to be honest there have been times when I wanted to give up on my marriage. But I, too, have come to realize a great marriage is a process. For some it takes a long time, but I'm convinced if we are faithful to follow God's definition of how to love another, God will honor our marriages.

In her book *How to Act Right When Your Spouse Acts Wrong*, Leslie Vernick writes,

As we center our heart in God, we learn to acknowledge and accept His sovereign control over every circumstance in our life—including our marriage. God never promises us that we will not experience troubles in this life; in fact, He tells us just the opposite (John 16:33). He never tells us that nothing will ever hurt us or that we should look for the easiest way out of our difficulties. God promises this: First, that He will take every difficulty we encounter, including difficulties in our marriage and transform them into something that will help us become more like Jesus, which He tells us is very, very good (Romans 8:38–39). Second, He promises that nothing that happens to us will *ever* be able to separate us from His love. *Ever!* He is in control and always sees the big picture.[1]

The big picture, that's exactly what God sees. God sees our lives from beginning to end and all in between. God can work good from bad, but we have to be patient enough to realize that God always does His work in His timing. We live in a quick fix, microwave society, and we like things fixed FedEx fast. We want solutions to our problems now. Why do you think women's magazine covers always contain fast answers to the troubles that most women face. "Diet Busters: Lose Ten Pounds in Ten Days," or "Relationship Menders: Three Easy Steps to Reconciliation," or "Organize Your Home in One Hour or Less." You won't find quick and easy solutions here, because we can't find them in God's Word.

In Ephesians 4:2 Paul instructs us, "Be completely humble and gentle; be patient, bearing with one another in love." Peter encourages us to, "love each other deeply, because love covers over a multitude of sins" (1 Peter 4:8). The only way for us to be patient, love the unloving, and stay with our commitment is to have a heart that is surrendered and filled with God's love.

Easy? Not at all. God honoring? Oh yes. Marriage mending? Absolutely. With God all things are possible.

In Matthew 5:6, as part of His Sermon on the Mount, Jesus instructed, "Blessed are those who hunger and thirst for righteousness, for they will be filled." If we hunger and thirst for a husband who always acts right, then we may go hungry our whole lives. If on the other hand God is what we hunger and thirst for, then we will be filled to overflowing. Proverbs 21:21 encourages us, "He who pursues righteousness and love finds life, prosperity and honor."

The lady I referred to at the beginning just celebrated her

twentieth wedding anniversary. She told me, "If I would have given up ten years ago, another lady would be his wife today and benefiting from my tears and prayers all those years. And I would have missed out on an amazing marriage."

RELATIONSHIP BUILDER—*Write a covenant for both you and your husband to sign that says, "Divorce is not an option ever." Let's eliminate that word from our vocabulary.*

 THOUGHT FOR THE DAY—*"I hate divorce," says the LORD God of Israel.*—*[MALACHI 2:16]*

CHAPTER 23

EVEN IF . . .

As I write these words our nation is in shock over the horrible events that took place on September 11, 2001. So much happened that tragic day. So many memories are seared into the hearts of Americans. Scenes of explosions and devastation. Scenes of dust-covered people running for their lives. Scenes of brave firefighters and police officers risking their lives to help save others. Scenes of heartbroken people walking the streets of New York City looking for their missing loved ones. Scenes of rows and rows of pictures of those missing with phone numbers and pleas for someone with any information to call.

I sat in my living room that terrible day and the days following so deeply saddened for our country and especially for the thousands who lost loved ones. Then as personal stories started to surface our hearts were touched in an even deeper way. I'll never forget President Bush honoring Lisa Beamer, wife of killed airline passenger Todd Beamer. He and a few other passengers stood up against the hijackers and gave their lives to prevent the plane from crashing into another building. When I saw Lisa being interviewed, it was obvious she was sad but she had an eternal perspective that she would see her husband again in heaven. She so honored her late husband in the way she spoke of the wonderful character he displayed in everyday life even unto death. What touched me in Lisa's story was her confident resolve that this was God's perfect will and that she would honor her husband by going on with life.

That was the sentiment of many of the victims' families: though their hearts were broken, life would go on. And life has. Life has gone on but no one is the same as before September 11, 2001. At least I hope not. I hope all of our perspectives have changed for the better.

When you first heard of the tragedy, did you instantly want to gather your family all together at home and hug them while telling them how much you loved them? I know I did. Something in me clicked that said life is short and fragile. I think this same sentiment clicked with a lot of people. Reports surfaced that in record numbers people on track to divorce notified the court system that they were giving their marriages one more chance. Many people took a step back from their busy lives and thought about what really matters.

What really matters with your marriage? I think about some of the little things that frustrate me, and I have to ask, does it really matter? Does it really matter that he sometimes leaves the toilet seat up? Does it really matter that he sets his dirty dinner plate on the counter beside the sink instead of rinsing it and putting it in the dishwasher? Does it really matter that we have differing opinions on this matter or that? The little things that we sometimes let chip away at our marriage would quickly fade if we kept the perspective that we've been blessed with today but are never guaranteed tomorrow.

One of the surveys I received back from men really stood out to me. One said, "I wish my wife knew that everyone makes mistakes and deserves a second chance."

The other quote said this, "I wish my wife understood how truly fragile I am as a man even though I won't show it. When she responds to me and supports me, I can do anything through Christ. But when she is insensitive it is devastating to me. I won't show it and usually I'll react by becoming 'hard,' but I'm crying out on the inside. She has no idea how much her belief and support means to me" (Tim, Tupelo). This man is calling out to his wife to be his helpmate, his support, his friend, the one who believes in him through thick and thin.

Does your husband know that if you had to do it all over again, you'd still choose him? Even if he lost everything financially. Even if he were paralyzed tomorrow. Even if he made a bad choice, you'd still choose him. Being able to answer yes to these questions today will bless your husband, but it will bless you even more. This is what it means to live without regrets. If these issues are resolved in your heart today, then should tragedy strike tomorrow, you'd have the full assurance that you gave and loved and lived life to the fullest, without regret, having given the good answer to all the even fs.

RELATIONSHIP BUILDER—*Find a tree in your yard and carve yours and your husband's initials into it. Carve a heart around the initials. After dinner take a nature walk to let your family discover the sweet inscription.*

 THOUGHT FOR THE DAY—*She has no idea how much her belief and support means to me.*—TIM [TUPELO]

CHAPTER 24

HAPPILY EVER AFTER

D o happily-ever-afters exist in our world today? All the statistics tell us that for a marriage to stay together in this day and age is rare. Last Sunday my pastor, Rob Singleton, preached a sermon on marriage and started by telling us two words that grated on his nerves like few others: soul mate. He's had one too many counseling sessions with people leaving their spouses because they finally found the *soul mate* they can't live without. In other words the grass seems greener on the other side and so they want to jump the fence and abandon their marriage commitment. He then gave us this quote, which I love: "The grass isn't greener on that side or this side. The grass is greener where you water and fertilize it." How true.

I can't think of a better way to water and fertilize our marriages than with the Word of God. Scripture is full of wisdom concerning our relationships and God's design for a good marriage. In my Bible (*The NIV Life Application Study Bible*), there is a list of many verses outlining God's intention for marriage.[1] As I studied these verses, I thought it most appropriate to share some of them with you. Because God's Word is alive and life-changing, I believe these verses will have a powerful effect on the way you approach your marriage from now on; they certainly helped me.

MARRIAGE IS GOD'S IDEA: GENESIS 2:18, 21–22

"The LORD God said, 'It is not good for the man to be alone. I will make a helper suitable for him.' . . . So the LORD God caused the man to fall into a deep sleep; and while he was sleeping, he took one of the man's ribs and closed up the place with flesh. Then the LORD God made a woman from the rib he had taken out of the man, and he brought her to the man."

Of all the things God made while forming the earth and everything in it, the only time the Lord said something was not good was when Adam was the only human. It was not good because the picture was not complete. Eve became Adam's completer creating a beautiful picture of the oneness God intended for us to experience in our marriages. It was never created to cause us heartache or trouble, but like everything else in our fallen world, our marriage relationships become tainted with sin. Selfishness comes into the picture from both partners and can wreak havoc on a relationship. Sometimes we may get so discouraged as to think marriage was a bad idea. God has never had a bad idea. Marriage is good because it was God's idea. If your marriage is not good, as mine was not for years, go to God and ask Him to show you how to make it better.

COMMITMENT IS ESSENTIAL: GENESIS 24:58–60

"So they called Rebekah and asked her, 'Will you go with this man?' 'I will go,' she said. So they sent their sister Rebekah on her way, along with her nurse and Abraham's servant and his men. And

they blessed Rebekah and said to her, 'Our sister, may you increase to thousands upon thousands; may your offspring possess the gates of their enemies.'

There have been many times where I did not want to answer as Rebekah; that I would go with this man. In fact I've wanted to run in the opposite direction at times! The only thing that kept me from running was my relationship with God and my commitment to honor Him. I'm glad I've stayed true to my commitment because just like Rebekah, I've been blessed beyond measure.

Notice the blessing didn't come until she verbally committed to going with her man and started on her way. Let me encourage you, even if you've found yourself pulling away from your husband and waning in your desire to stay committed, blessings are ahead if you stay true to honoring God in your marriage. Determine today to take the first steps toward positive actions.

ROMANCE IS IMPORTANT: SONG OF SOLOMON 4:9–10

"You have stolen my heart, my sister, my bride; you have stolen my heart with one glance of your eyes, with one jewel of your necklace. How delightful is your love, my sister, my bride! How much more pleasing is your love than wine, and the fragrance of your perfume than any spice!"

We read these verses in a previous chapter but how

encouraging they are. Don't you long to hear these words from your husband? Maybe that's why you've picked up this book to learn how to capture his heart in such a way that he says words like these often. We've learned a lot about keeping the romance alive in our marriages through these pages. Keep the ideas flowing and continue to stoke the flames of passion in your relationship. Determine to become a romantic at heart.

MARRIAGE IS BASED ON PRINCIPLED PRACTICE OF LOVE: EPHESIANS 5:22, 25, 33

"Wives submit to your husbands as to the LORD. . . . Husbands, love your wives, just as Christ loved the church and gave himself up for her. . . . each one of you also must love his wife as he loves himself, and the wife must respect her husband."

Isn't it interesting that there are no qualifying statements surrounding these verses? There are no statements like: "when your husband is nice you should respect him," or "when you are sure he's making a good decision, submit to him." God instructs us to respect and submit—to practice these principles of love because they honor God. If we only base our actions on our feelings, we will miss the mark of God's plan for our marriage.

So back to my original question: do happily-ever-afters still exist? Let me leave you with one verse that I think assures us when we follow God's plan they absolutely do. "There will be heard once more the sounds of joy and gladness, the voices of bride and bridegroom, and the voices of those who bring thank offerings to the house of the LORD, saying, 'Give thanks to the LORD Almighty, for the LORD is good; his love endures forever'" (Jeremiah 33:10–11).

RELATIONSHIP BUILDER—*Memorize Jeremiah 33:10–11 to encourage you. Quote it often.*

 THOUGHT FOR THE DAY—*If we only base our actions on our feelings, we will miss the mark of God's plan for our marriage.*—*[LYSA TERKEURST]*

NO MARRIAGE IS
PICTURE-PERFECT

I thought it was a simple request: a photo shoot. I needed a picture by myself for another project and one of Art and me together for this book. Art and I met at the photo studio and started thumbing through the photographer's example books. "Wow, this type of picture is nice," I said as I held it up for the photographer to see. I continued, "I'm the author of a couple of marriage books, so we're here to get a photo for the back of my book."

"Oh, I see," he said with a concerned look on his face. "Now you weren't thinking of an outside picture today were you?"

"Well, actually I'd like one like this one," I said, a little shaky as I showed him a picture of a couple standing in a grassy field.

"Those kinds of pictures take more planning than your standard inside session. If you wanted one like that, we should have thought about it a little more in advance," he said with eyebrows raised.

"Oh, okay a studio picture it is then," I said, feeling a little hurt and a lot disappointed.

"Very well then, what coordinating clothes did you bring and we'll pick a background color that will contrast nicely," he said.

Suddenly the knot in my stomach twisted and grew quite

large as I held up what we were planning to wear and the photographer made his disapproval clear. All the while Art is standing off to the side with an I-told-you look on his face that was making me more upset by the minute. He didn't want to get the pictures taken that day in the first place. He thought we needed to take a couple of weeks to plan things. Plus he wanted to get a haircut. I thought a couple days' notice was plenty of time. Let's just go, smile nicely, and check it off the to-do list was my thought process. I was now in no mood to smile so we rescheduled.

Therefore the picture you see on the back cover that appears to be my husband and me is actually another couple . . . just kidding.

We rescheduled the picture session for the next week and went out to the parking lot. I was angry. Art is always reminding me we shouldn't try to do things last minute. Most of the time it all just somehow works out but not this time. I was stewin', fussin', and fumin'. Photo hair takes time, not to mention the makeup and accessories and the many prayers to ward off unsightly blemishes. Isn't that just like life though? We want things to be picture-perfect and inevitably they never are.

This is especially true with our marriages. We dream about finally meeting that someone special who is going to make our life wonderful and then a wedding and a couple of kids later we feel disillusioned and disappointed. Why? Our hearts were made for the Garden of Eden but life is more like the Garden of Gethsemane.

We were made for perfect peace, perfect provision, perfect surroundings, and perfect love. Our souls cry in anguish at times over this world's distortion of God's design. Instead of turning to God and letting His perfect peace, provision, and love fill our empty places, we kick into fix-it mode. We strategize. We manipulate. We set agendas. We search out a three-step method to "change him."

We wear ourselves out only to come to the end of our emotional and physical ropes and realize that despite all our efforts there is no human answer. Our hope lies solely in Jesus Christ and His plans for us. Jesus wants our marriages to be symbols of His unconditional and sacrificial love for His bride, the church. No wonder Satan wants to destroy our marriages. Ephesians 6 warns us that our struggles are not against flesh and blood but against evil forces.

Think back to all those fairytales that helped shape your thoughts of marriage. They always had a hero, a heroine, and some evil counterpart. So goes our story as well. It is my prayer that this book has helped encourage and equip you to strengthen your love for your husband and thwart the efforts of the evil one. Does this mean we'll never have another marital spat? No, but maybe our perspective will be different and our resolve to keep on going will be strengthened.

Recently, I was speaking at a church retreat where the pastor's wife shared a story that will forever help me to press on. She told me of a dear young mother in their congregation who found out she had breast cancer. She fought the disease with all her might but her condition worsened. In an attempt to help save her, the doctors tried one final surgery. During the procedure her heart stopped, but after several attempts at reviving her the surgeons were able to bring her back. Though she survived the surgery, she was told shortly after she awoke that the cancer had spread and the prognosis was poor.

Upon hearing the surgeon's report, she gathered her family and many of her friends in her hospital room. The ones who were there said though her body had wasted away and physically it was apparent she was close to the end, her spirit was so full of peace that she was radiantly beautiful. When they were all there, she told them that during the surgery she had died and the surgeons had had to work hard to bring her back. She did revive but not before seeing a glimpse of eternity. She told them she had not been allowed to see Jesus' face but she had seen enough to know that everything the Bible promised it would be *is* true. "It's all true," she said as she smiled and told them goodbye.

It is all true, my friend. Though they may not make sense in the world's eyes, all of God's precepts and promises are true. Your husband is a gift that God has blessed you with for a time. Hold on tightly to God's Word and His design for your marriage. You will be incredibly blessed as you give your husband the gift of a godly wife who captures his heart.

RELATIONSHIP BUILDER—*In your marriage journal, write a thank you letter to God telling Him how much you appreciate your husband.*

 THOUGHT FOR THE DAY—*It's all true!*

NOTES

CHAPTER 2

1. Portions of this story first appeared in the *Proverbs 31 Woman* newsletter. It has been updated, condensed, and used by permission of Curt Whalen.
2. Nancy Groom, *Heart to Heart About Men* (Colorado Springs: NavPress, 1995), 45–46.
3. Ibid.

CHAPTER 3

1. Stormie Omartian, *The Power of a Praying Wife* (Eugene, Ore.: Harvest House, 1995), 17.

CHAPTER 4

1. Sister Mary Rose McGready, *Please Help Me God*.

CHAPTER 5

1. Stu Weber, *Four Pillars of a Man's Heart* (Sisters, Ore.: Multnomah, 1997), 258–59.

CHAPTER 6

1. John Eldredge, *Wild at Heart* (Nashville: Thomas Nelson, 2001), 9.
2. Ibid., 82.
3. Lance Morrow, "Men: Are They Really That Bad?" *Time,* 14 February 1994, 54.

CHAPTER 8

1. Robert and Rosemary Barnes, *Rock Solid Marriage* (Grand Rapids: Zondervan, 1996), 163.
2. Ibid, 165.
3. Portions of this chapter condensed from *Seven Life Principles for Every Woman* by Sharon Jaynes and Lysa TerKeurst (Chicago: Moody, 2001), 68–70.
4. Robert Lewis and William Hendricks, *Rocking the Roles* (Colorado Springs: NavPress, 1991), 117.

CHAPTER 9

1. Dr. Douglas Rosenau, *A Celebration of Sex* (Nashville: Thomas Nelson, 1994), 86.
2. Ibid. 91.
3. Robert and Rosemary Barnes, *Great Sexpectations* (Grand Rapids: Zondervan, 1996), 157.

CHAPTER 10

1. Commentary on Philippians 4:10–14 from *NIV Life Application Study Bible* (Wheaton and Grand Rapids: Tyndale and Zondervan, 1988), 2154.
2. Chuck Snyder, *Men: Some Assembly Required* (Colorado Springs: Focus on the Family, 1995), 35.

CHAPTER 11

1. Patrick Morley, *What Husbands Wish Their Wives Knew About Men* (Grand Rapids: Zondervan, 1998), 89.

CHAPTER 13

1. Lysa TerKeurst, *Capture Her Heart* (Chicago: Moody, 2002), 76.

CHAPTER 15

1. Robert Lewis and William Hendricks, *Rocking the Roles* (Colorado Springs: NavPress, 1991), 127.
2. Ibid.

CHAPTER 17

1. Bill and Pam Farrel, *Men Are Like Waffles, Women Are Like Spaghetti* (Eugene, Ore.: Harvest House, 2001), 11–12. Used by permission.
2. Ibid., 13.

CHAPTER 18

1. Nancy Cobb and Connie Grigsby, *How to Get Your Husband to Talk to You* (Sisters, Ore.: Multnomah, 2001), 241–42.

CHAPTER 19

1. Gregory J. P. Godek, *Romantic Dates* (Naperville, Ill.: Casablanca, 1997), 52–53.
2. Richard Restak, M.D., *The Brain* (New York: Bantam, 1984), 242–45.
3. Gary Smalley and John Trent, *The Language of Love* (Pomona, Calif.: Focus on the Family, 1988), 35–36.
4. D. Kimura, "Early Motor Functions of the Left and Right Hemisphere," *Brain* 97: 337–50.
5. Robert Kohn, "Patterns of Hemispheric Specialization in Pre-Schoolers," *Neuropsychologia* 12:505–12.
6. J. Levy, "The Adaptive Advantages of Cerebral Asymmetry and Communication," *Annuals of the New York Academy of Sciences* 229:264–72.
7. Dr. James and Shirley Dobson, *Night Light* (Sisters, Ore.: Multnomah, 2000), 201.
8. Ibid.

CHAPTER 20

1. Dave and Jan Dravecky with Ken Gire, *When You Can't Come Back* (Grand Rapids and San Francisco: Zondervan and Harper Collins, 1992), 126–27.

CHAPTER 21

1. John Eldridge, *Wild at Heart* (Nashville: Thomas Nelson, 2001), 192.
2. Patrick Morley, *What Husbands Wish Their Wives Knew About Men* (Grand Rapids: Zondervan, 1998), 172–73.
3. Chuck Snyder, *Men: Some Assembly Required* (Colorado Springs: Focus on the Family, 1995), 34.

CHAPTER 22

1. Leslie Vernick, *How to Act Right When Your Spouse Acts Wrong* (Colorado Springs: Waterbrook, 2001), 99.

CHAPTER 24

1. "What the Bible Says About Marriage," *NIV Life Application Study Bible* (Wheaton and Grand Rapids: Tyndale and Zondervan, 1988), 9.

Art and Lysa TerKeurst are available for marriage conferences and seminars. To inquire about booking them together for a speaking engagement or to inquire about having Lysa speak to your group, contact:

Proverbs 31 Ministries

PO Box 17155

Charlotte, NC 28227

1-877-731-4663

http://www.proverbs31.org/

or e-mail: office@Proverbs31.org

ABOUT PROVERBS 31 MINISTRIES

Proverbs 31 Ministries is a nondenominational organization dedicated to glorifying God by touching women's hearts to build godly homes. Through Jesus Christ, we shed light on God's distinctive design for women and the great responsibilities we have been given. With Proverbs 31:10–31 as a guide, we encourage and equip women to practice living out their faith as wives, mothers, friends, and neighbors.

What began in 1992 as a monthly newsletter has now grown into a multifaceted ministry reaching women across the country and around the globe. Each aspect of the ministry seeks to equip women in the Seven Principles of *The Proverbs 31 Woman.*

1. The Proverbs 31 woman reveres Jesus Christ as Lord of her life and pursues an ongoing, personal relationship with Him.

2. The Proverbs 31 woman loves, honors, and respects her husband as the leader of the home.

3. The Proverbs 31 woman nurtures her children and believes that motherhood is a high calling with the responsibility of shaping and molding the children who will one day define who we are as a community and a nation.

4. The Proverbs 31 woman is a disciplined and industrious keeper of the home who creates a warm and loving environment for her family and friends.

5. The Proverbs 31 woman contributes to the financial well-being of her household by being a faithful steward of the time and money God has entrusted to her.

6. The Proverbs 31 woman speaks with wisdom and faithful instruction as she mentors and supports other women and develops godly friendships.

7. The Proverbs 31 woman shares the love of Christ by extending her hands to help with the needs in the community.

MINISTRY FEATURES

NEWSLETTER—The Proverbs 31 Woman is a twelve-page, monthly publication, which is a storehouse of inspiration and information to equip women in the seven principles of the Proverbs 31 woman.

RADIO MINISTRY—The Proverbs 31 Radio Ministry airs a daily two-minute program heard on approximately four hundred networks across the country and overseas.

SPEAKING MINISTRY—The Proverbs 31 Ministry features

dynamic speakers who share life-changing and inspirational messages at women's conferences, banquets, and retreats.

ON-LINE SUPPORT GROUP—Through the Internet, this support group includes an on-line Bible study and book club for women who may not otherwise have an opportunity for fellowship.

ENCOURAGEMENT GROUPS—Women in churches around the country enjoy the benefits of small group Bible study and fellowship at their church, home, or office. These groups are chartered through Proverbs 31 Ministry.

SHE SPEAKS—Proverbs 31 Ministries offers training and certification for women to become Proverbs 31 speakers. If God has called you to the podium, call us!

For a sample issue of our newsletter, or more information on the ministry, write or call:

The Proverbs 31 Ministry
PO Box 17155
Charlotte, NC 28227

PROVERBS · 31
MINISTRIES

877-p31-home (877-731-4663)
web site: www.proverbs31.org

Moody Press, a ministry of Moody Bible Institute,

is designed for education, evangelization, and edification.

If we may assist you in knowing more about Christ

and the Christian life, please write us without obligation:

Moody Press, c/o MLM, Chicago, Illinois 60610.

CAPTURE HIS HEART

EIGHT-WEEK
STUDY GROUP QUESTIONS

his book can be used as material for a women's study group. Whether you are in an accountability group or a ladies' Bible study, *Capture His Heart* will aid in helpful discussions as you learn together to make your marriage all God intends it to be. It is crucial that everything discussed within this group be held in the strictest of confidence. This group exists to encourage one another in the pursuit of godly marriages and to lift one another up in prayer.

YOUR HUSBAND NEEDS YOU TO SUPPORT HIM SPIRITUALLY
Chapters 1–3

1. What are some of our deep spiritual needs as women?

2. Why is it so important to get every spiritual need met by God alone? What happens when we try to make our husbands meet our every need?

3. How were you encouraged by Curt Whalen's story?

4. Comment on Susan Yates's quote: "A woman will do whatever she can to control a man, but if she succeeds, she won't be happy."

5. Why is prayer so powerful in a marriage?

6. Which relationship builder had the most impact on your husband this week?

YOUR HUSBAND NEEDS YOU TO ENCOURAGE HIM EMOTIONALLY
Chapters 4–6

1. How could serving and loving your husband as if you were doing it for Jesus change your perspective?

2. Why is it important to realize our husbands have tender spots? How could we better understand their vulnerabilities?

3. Discuss John Eldridge's quote of the three main desires of a man's heart: "a battle to fight, an adventure to live, and a beauty to rescue."

4. What does your husband love to do that expresses his masculinity? How could you better support him in this?

5. Why does it negatively affect the passion of a relationship when a man becomes completely domesticated?

6. Which relationship builder had the most impact on your husband this week?

YOUR HUSBAND NEEDS YOU TO ENJOY HIM SEXUALLY
Chapters 7–9

1. Why do you think the words, "effort, enthusiastic, and desire" were so common in the surveys turned in from men wanting their wives to enjoy them sexually?

2. Why is it important for our husbands to know they are wholly desirable and acceptable?

3. What are the benefits that God intends husbands and wives to experience through intimacy?

4. How does a woman's desire for unconditional love affect her desire to be intimate with her husband? Who is the only one who can love her unconditionally?

5. How can strengthening our relationship with the Lord and reading His Word help intimate issues in marriages?

6. Which relationship builder had the most impact on your husband this week?

YOUR HUSBAND NEEDS YOU TO APPRECIATE HIM VOCATIONALLY
Chapters 10–12

1. Why is perspective so important in determining whether or not we are content? How does our discontentment affect our provider?

2. What are some other practical ways to puff up our provider?

3. Why is a wife's influence so important in determining her husband's success at work and at home?

4. What are some creative things you've done to turn your house into a haven?

5. Comment on this statement: "When you bless your husband, you receive a great blessing yourself."

6. Which relationship builder had the most impact on your husband this week?

YOUR HUSBAND NEEDS YOU TO
ENGAGE HIM INTELLECTUALLY
Chapters 13–15

1. Can you relate to speaking in "hints"?

2. How can we make our requests to our husbands simple and nonemotional?

3. How does the filter of past hurts negatively affect a marriage?

4. Why is it important for husbands and wives to share their dreams?

5. Have you seen the powerful effect of helping your husband realize a dream?

6. Which relationship builder had the most impact on your husband this week?

YOUR HUSBAND NEEDS YOU TO CONNECT WITH HIM RELATIONALLY
Chapters 16–18

1. Why is it important to maintain the thrill of discovery in a marriage?

2. How can we get creative and set aside times to have in-depth conversations with our husbands? How will this help our marriage relationships grow and deepen?

3. How can understanding the different ways men and women process information help communication with our husbands?

4. Discuss the waffle/spaghetti analogy and how this affects our communication with our spouses.

5. Why is learning to laugh with each other key to unlocking the friendship facet of a marriage?

6. Which relationship builder had the most impact on your husband this week?

YOUR HUSBAND NEEDS YOU TO
AFFIRM HIM PHYSICALLY
Chapters 19–21

1. Why do you think God designed men and women to be so
   different?

2. How can these differences work to help our relationships
   and not harm them?

3. Read "Habakkuk 3 for Marriage" and discuss how we can
   keep this perspective.

4. How is a man's heart drawn out by a woman's beauty?

5. Describe a woman with a gentle and quiet spirit. Does
   this mean she has to be quiet all the time?

6. Which relationship builder had the most impact on your
   husband this week?

YOUR HUSBAND NEEDS YOU TO STAND BY HIM PERMANENTLY
Chapters 22–24

1. Why is it important to realize marriage is a process worth persevering?

2. How does Matthew 5:6 apply to our marriages?

3. How does asking, "Does it really matter?" help put aggravations into perspective?

4. Do happily-ever-afters exist? How can we find a real happily ever after ending?

5. Comment on this statement: "Marriage is based on the principled practice of love, not on feelings."

6. Which relationship builder had the most impact on your husband this week?

FOCUS ON THE FAMILY®

Welcome to the Family!

Whether you received this book as a gift, borrowed it from a friend, or purchased it yourself, we're glad you read it! It's just one of the many helpful, insightful, and encouraging resources produced by Focus on the Family.

In fact, that's what Focus on the Family is all about—providing inspiration, information, and biblically based advice to people in all stages of life.

It began in 1977 with the vision of one man, Dr. James Dobson, a licensed psychologist and author of 16 best-selling books on marriage, parenting, and family. Alarmed by the societal, political, and economic pressures that were threatening the existence of the American family, Dr. Dobson founded Focus on the Family with one employee—an assistant—and a once-a-week radio broadcast, aired on only 36 stations.

Now an international organization, Focus on the Family is dedicated to preserving Judeo-Christian values and strengthening the family through more than 70 different ministries, including eight separate daily radio broadcasts; television public service announcements; 10 publications; and a steady series of books and award-winning films and videos for people of all ages and interests.

Recognizing the needs of, as well as the sacrifices and important contributions made by, such diverse groups as educators, physicians, attorneys, crisis pregnancy center staff, and single parents, Focus on the Family offers specific outreaches to uphold and minister to these individuals, too. And it's all done for one purpose, and one purpose only: to encourage and strengthen individuals and families through the life-changing message of Jesus Christ.

• • •

For more information about the ministry, or if we can be of help to your family, simply write to Focus on the Family, Colorado Springs, CO 80995 or call 1-800-A-FAMILY (1-800-232-6459). Friends in Canada may write Focus on the Family, P.O. Box 9800, Stn. Terminal, Vancouver, B.C. V6B 4G3. or call 1-800-661-9800. Visit our Web site—www.family.org— to learn more about Focus on the Family or to find out if there is an associate office in your country.

We'd love to hear from you!

Other Faith and Family Strengtheners
From Focus on the Family ®

The Marriage Masterpiece takes a fresh appraisal of the exquisite design God has for a man and woman. Explaining the reasons why this union is meant to last a lifetime, it also shows how God's relationship with humanity is the model for marriage. Rediscover the beauty and worth of marriage in a new light with this thoughtful, creative book. A helpful study guide is included for group discussion. Available in hardcover and two-cassette album.

Learning to Live With the Love of Your Life— an encouraging and insightful book that offers practical guidelines for enhancing intimacy, communication and romance in your relationship. For both newlyweds and longtime mates, it's a powerful plan for holding on to the wonder and joy of love. Request it for yourself or as a gift for a couple you love. Available in hardcover and two-cassette album.

•   •   •

Look for these special books in your Christian bookstore or request a copy by calling 1-800-A-FAMILY (1-800-232-6459). Friends in Canada may write Focus on the Family, P.O. Box 9800, Stn. Terminal, Vancouver, B.C. V6B 4G3 or call 1-800-661-9800.

Visit our Web site (www.family.org) to learn more about the ministry or find out if there is a Focus on the Family office in your country.

Further Insights by Moody Press

CAPTURE HER HEART

Capture Her Heart is a practicle "tool box"
that will be a quick daily read that will open a
husband's eye's to the needs of his wife. It
will help him move past frustrations and into
a fullfilling marriage as he learns eight key
things every husbsnd should know.

ISBN: 0-8024-4040-1

WHO HOLDS THE KEY TO YOUR HEART?

Inside each of us lies a secret place, hidden from the view of out-
siders. The truth is God knows the secrets
of your heart and He is waiting for you to
give them to Him.

Who Holds the Key to Your Heart? is your
map through the deepest places of your
soul, where God can reveal His truth and
set you free. Once He unlocks every hurting and dark place, He will then offer you
hope, heal you with God's Word and fill you
with His redeeming love, joy and peace!

ISBN: 0-8024-3310-3

MOODY
The Name You Can Trust®
1-800-678-8812 www.MoodyPress.org

Further Insights by Moody Press

Seven Life Principles for Every Women

In society today, boundaries are blurred, roles are reversed and priorities perplex us. Do you feel like you need to bring your life into focus and achieve some sense of balance? Look no further!

"Sharon and Lysa have captured the heart of what it means to be a woman of God. With wisdom, warmth, and wit they present a compelling vision of the high calling that is ours as women. Their rich practical insights are solidly rooted in the Scripture and engagingly illustrated out of their own lives." - Nancy LeDeMoss

ISBN: 0-8024-3398-7

Living Life On Purpose

Every women longs to live up to her full, God-given potential. But the hectic nature of your life may leave you struggling just to keep your head above water. Fortunately, you can do more than simply survive. These two books can guide you in developing a Life Plan. More than just helping you get a better handle on your schedule, your Life Plan will allow you to enjoy a life that is truly well-lived

ISBN: 0-8024-4195-5